WHAT PEOPLE ARE
MY LORD AND MY GOD

'Practical, challenging, accessible and inspiring. A wonderful look at the life of Thomas and the clear lessons from him for those of us wanting to share the gospel today. Get it and live it!' – *Gavin Calver, CEO, Evangelical Alliance*

'Ben's inimitable style is found throughout this practical and insightful book, which will be a fantastic resource to pass on to others. It's a great insight into discovering what it means to follow Jesus. I strongly recommend it!' – *Roy Crowne, Director, HOPE Together*

'Working with Ben on launching Advance groups around the globe has been a tremendous blessing as we seek to stir the church to evangelism and to promote and develop the calling of evangelists in their efforts to proclaim the gospel. I know that you will find this profoundly encouraging and inspiring book (and future instalments in this series) a timely read filled with timeless truth as we head into a doubt-filled world for the glory of Jesus.' – *Desmond Henry, Director, Global Network of Evangelists*

'Doubt is a part of the human condition, and here my friend Ben Jack challenges us to move through this "inevitable consequence of our human frailty" to the joy of encountering the living God in the face of Jesus. Ben uses the life of the apostle Thomas as a lens to help us deepen our devotion to a Christ we can know and experience. I challenge you to read this book and see it as an invitation to join the untold millions who, like Thomas, move from fear and doubt to full, joyful devotion.' – *Kevin Palau, President and CEO, Luis Palau Association*

'It's so refreshing to read a book that is anchored in a theme, a character and a Bible passage, and then from there explodes in so many directions you've never thought about – immensely stimulating, not least because it's laced with real-life stories.' – *Rico Tice, Associate Minister, All Soul's Langham Place and founder, Christianity Explored Ministries*

'This book is just brilliant and full of divine gems! Writing with genuine humility, Ben Jack offers a powerful revelation that, even with our human limitations, we can be assured of the great hope of what God's work in and through us can achieve. How beautiful to read a book about Thomas, the one who "failed" by doubting, but also the disciple I can most easily identify with because I often experience doubt too. The time of the religious superstar – the superhero "professional Christian" – is over, and this book will help ordinary followers of Jesus step into the extraordinary life he has for each of us to serve him day by day. Read on and take up the invitation to humbly listen to Jesus as he calls us to "be faithless no more and believe," to be led to our knees where we can cry out in response, "My Lord and my God."' – *Jean-Luc Trachsel, Europe Shall Be Saved and Co-chair, Global Evangelists Alliance*

MY LORD AND MY GOD

MY LORD AND MY GOD

AN INVITATION TO DEVOTION FOR A WORLD IN DOUBT

BEN JACK

© by Ben Jack 2020

Published by Equipping the Church, a brand of Kingsway CLC Trust,
Unit 5, Glendale Avenue, Sandycroft, Deeside, CH5 2QP

Kingsway CLC Trust is a registered Charity, Number 265612, and a Limited
Company registered in registered in England, Registration Number 1093879

The right of Ben Jack to be identified as the author of this work has been asserted
by him in accordance with the Copyright, Designs and Patents Act 1988

Unless otherwise indicated, all Scripture references are taken from NIV: New
International Version® Anglicised, NIV® Copyright © 1979, 1984, 2011
by Biblica, Inc.® Used by permission, all rights reserved worldwide.

Concept development by The Message Trust
Cover design and typesetting by Simon Baker at Thirteen Creative
Author photograph by Rachael Silvester

Every effort has been made to ensure that this book contains correct
permissions and references, but if anything has been inadvertently
overlooked the Publisher will be pleased to make the necessary arrangements
at the first opportunity. Please contact the Publisher directly.

Printed in the EU
ISBN: 978-1-8381704-0-0

For Old Tom,
another Thomas who has taught me so much
about what it means to faithfully live out
the words 'my Lord and my God.'

CONTENTS

INTRODUCTION TO THE ADVANCE PROCLAIMERS SERIES

The Bible is full of proclamation. From its very beginning we encounter a God who speaks – a God who literally proclaims the universe, and us along with it, into existence.

Throughout scripture, God continues to speak in various ways, most frequently through his people making proclamations about him and on his behalf. We are eventually confronted with Jesus Christ, whose life, teaching, death and resurrection proclaim a message of hope to the world. It's a message that is still being heard today, especially where God's people – the church – continue to proclaim his truth.

The *Advance Proclaimers Series* (APS) helps readers engage with specific moments of proclamation in the Bible, so that we may grow in our understanding of the truth being declared, grow in our knowledge of how to apply it to our own lives, and grow in our confidence to proclaim its truth to our world.

Each title in the series uses a single clear proclamation from the Bible as the starting point for a thematic study that is committed to accurate exposition of scripture, a readable and engaging style of writing and a clear evangelistic application for the reader.

Bible verses, sources and further comment have been placed in the notes section at the end of this book to keep the main text clear, readable and succinct. At the end of each chapter, you will also find discussion questions and a practical application which you can use either for personal reflection or for group discussion.

We hope that this series is an encouragement to you as you explore, consider and act upon God's call to evangelism for his church. We pray that together we would discover God's truth through the pages of scripture and go into the world as proclaimers of that truth today.

To find out more about the *Advance Proclaimers Series* and to discover other titles, visit **advancegroups.org/aps**.

Desmond Henry and Ben Jack
Series Editors

PROLOGUE

If you're anything like me then your favourite Bible character probably changes over time – perhaps depending on which parts of the Bible you've been reading recently, or the season of life you're in.[1] Feeling like a bit of a failure? We might be drawn to King David or the apostle Peter as we hope to be reassured by the wonder of God's restoration. Finding yourself inspired by those who exhibit outrageous courage? The stories about Esther, Daniel, or Stephen are all challenging and encouraging no matter how many times we read them. Experiencing persecution for your lack of hair? Elisha is effectively a superhero figure for the follicularly oppressed (fortunately for my taunters, God has yet to unleash the bears I've requested).[2]

Despite a long list of fluctuating favourites over the years, there is one of Jesus' first disciples who continues to intrigue me. While Peter would likely get top billing and the most lines in a film about the not-so-dirty dozen, and John may have thought of himself as Jesus' favourite, my favourite is actually Thomas.

I know what you're thinking. Really? The doubting guy? Surely he's too much of a cynic for an optimistic evangelist like you?[3] Not at all!

Aside from Judas and the big three (great band name by the way) – Peter, James and John – Thomas is the disciple who is mentioned the most in the gospels.[4] But for my money he's the most misunderstood, not least because of the infamous nickname that we've given him – doubting Thomas. While we should always be careful in attempting to paint full characters based only on the brief snapshots of their lives we find in the Bible, in Thomas' appearances I find a relatable, adventurous, Jesus-loving world-changer.[5] He is a man who moved from doubt to devotion to become the first person in the New Testament to proclaim (and worship) Jesus as his Lord and his God. He was a man who, along with the other disciples, would go on to courageously and sacrificially take the gospel to the nations, and in so doing play a critical role in the transformation of the entire world.

In the first part of this book we will see how the brokenness and isolation Thomas experienced after Jesus' crucifixion, and the mischaracterisation of his identity that has followed, finds a parallel with many people in today's world, and we will explore how we might offer those people the truth, power and hope of the gospel.

In the second part we will discover through Thomas' relationship with Jesus what it means for a person to respond appropriately to the risen Christ – with hope-filled worship, trust in his word, and world-changing witness.

Even though Thomas is the inspiration for this book, he is not its ultimate focus. The following pages give testimony to Jesus Christ – the one who, when doubt threatened to crush, stepped in to provoke Thomas' staggering confession. And it's the very same confession that we all are to worshipfully profess with our lips and our lives as each of us discovers that Jesus is 'my Lord and my God.'

PART ONE
THE WORLD

ONE
DOUBTING

Then he said to Thomas, 'Put your finger here;
see my hands. Reach out your hand and put it
into my side. Stop doubting and believe.'
JOHN 20:27

Have you ever been given a nickname that you didn't like? Nicknames often originate as a comment on a person's appearance or particular behaviour. Coming in a little under the average height? Nice to meet you, Short Round.[6] Do you regularly bore...sorry...*bless* your friends with facts and figures? Hey, Statto. Always the first to bail on a social engagement because of a little sniffle? Get well soon, Sicknote!

Storytellers often use nicknames as a way to reinforce and remind us of something essential or defining about a character. 'Maverick' is the call sign of Tom Cruise's character in the movie *Top Gun*, and guess what? He is a maverick![7] Then there's 'Doc' Brown in *Back To The Future* (he's a scientist!), 'Data' in *The Goonies* (he's the techy gadget kid!), and Rocky in, erm, *Rocky* (he's a boxer like Rocky Marciano!).[8] Apparently there are also films not made in the 70s or 80s but life is too short for all that.

Nicknames can be a way for friends and family to demonstrate their closeness and affection to you, even (perhaps especially!) when the name is comically derogatory in some way. Then there are those who receive a nickname as a direct insult and carry the hurt of the connotation and the social consequences of its association with them forever. Imagine if every time you walked into a room people greeted you by saying, 'Hey, it's failure Steve!' or, 'Hi, depressing Lucy!' Being defined by your failure or weakness every time you were introduced would be a burden, no matter how thick-skinned you are.

We could give nicknames to lots of people in the Bible who failed in one way or another. But we don't refer to David as 'David the Adulterer,' call Peter 'Peter the Denier,' or name Paul 'Persecutor Paul,' despite how accurate those nicknames might be. We don't attach the term 'doubting' to any of the other disciples, despite the fact that we're told that Jesus lamented Peter's doubt as he pulled him from the waves, and that, like Thomas, all the disciples seemed to doubt the resurrection at one time or another.[9] Yet here we are with 'doubting Thomas.'[10] Why the fascination? I suspect it might have something to do with the fact that experiencing doubt is part of what it means to be human.

ONE: DOUBTING

The television show *Who Do You Think You Are* invites celebrities (although they seem to play fast and loose with that definition) to explore their family history. In each episode the individual discovers hidden history and insights from their family tree, and in understanding more about their ancestors they often gain a fresh perspective on their own lives (hopefully without discovering any embarrassing skeletons in the family history closet on national television).

Each of us in some way asks the basic question: 'Who do I think I am?' The answers we come up with can have a profound effect on the way we live our lives. How we draw our conclusion is likely to be informed by our upbringing, our culture, what people say about us (including the nicknames they give us), our achievements and so on. But if we really want to know the true answer to our identity question we need to go beyond the names spoken over us, to look beyond the boundaries of our own lives – beyond our own doubt – and delve deeper into our history than a few generations of the family tree. We need to go all the way back to the creator of the universe.

The greatest problem the world faces today is one of identity crisis. People don't know *who* they are because they don't know *whose* they are. When you don't know where you've come from you'll never know where you're going, or for that matter, why any of it matters along the way. Foundations are important.

When we find our place in God's story rather than as the main attraction of our own mini-epic, everything changes. We get a new perspective on what it means to be human. We have the opportunity to move from mere existence into true life. Yet even those who know and love God find themselves struggling to make sense of the truth at times. We can still find ourselves being drawn back into the misunderstanding of yesterday, as today's challenges bring confusion to the journey and cause us to question the foundation of our lives.

In *Doubt: A History*, atheist historian and philosopher Jennifer Michael Hecht explores the experiences of doubters throughout history – including Job, who ranted at God, and St Augustine, who tore at his hair in his *Confessions* – and concludes that doubt itself can be as strong a foundation for our lives as faith:

> Throughout history, many great thinkers have argued that the study of these questions could give life meaning, grace, and happiness… The only thing such doubters really need, that believers have, is a sense that people like themselves have always been around, that they are part of a grand history.[11]

But is that really the best foundation we can hope for? To create meaning for ourselves through a shared experience of not knowing what this life is? Does anyone really take comfort in the idea that the only reliable truth is that no one else has ever known the truth either?

God offers us a better way, a better foundation. He invites us to examine our doubt by reasoning with him, to investigate his truth and put it to the test in our lives.[12] God invites us to build our lives on the solid foundation of the unchanging truth we discover. He invites us to know him with our heart, soul and mind – all we are – so that he would become our secure and life-giving foundation.

As Christians, when we wrestle with doubt we ask questions of God, but resolve to come out the other side in submission to his higher perspective and perfect will. The reality of being a finite creature exploring an infinite and transcendent God is that we will always find ourselves caught up in some kind of divine mystery. With that in mind (and to riff on Plato) 'the unexamined *faith* is not worth living,' for as we examine and test our faith there is hope to grow ever more confident in the goodness of God's foundation upon which we build.

As Hecht points out, Saint Augustine wrestled violently with his own doubts. But he didn't stay there. Eventually, his doubt would come to an end as he chose to place his full trust in Jesus – even before he found answers to all his questions, or release from his inner struggles. Many see this same process of wrestling with doubt as an important part of the Christian journey, but not a process without hope of an end where all shadows of doubt would disappear. As Paul puts it, 'Now I know in part; then I shall know fully.'[13]

Doubt is neither a foundation to build upon or an end in itself. Doubt is simply the inevitable consequence of our human frailty as we journey towards the ultimate foundation of God's truth. And it can be exchanged for something better as we encounter the living God. It can be exchanged for confident hope.[14]

It's good to ask questions. But when we use those questions to deconstruct the life-giving foundation of God, they can easily become the tools we use to construct a new foundation for our lives that has little to do with God's truth and more to do with ourselves. We find examples of this throughout the Bible, but here are three that are particularly helpful.

First let's go back to the very beginning – to the original doubters themselves, Adam and Eve. Everything is well in the garden of Eden. God's creation is perfect, and Adam and Eve are in perfect relationship with their creator. Then the snake (Satan, whose name means 'the accuser') comes along and points out the one tree in the garden from which they are forbidden to eat. With a simple sentence, he introduces doubt.

'Did God *really* say you can't eat from that tree?'[15]

And the rest, as they say, is sinful history.

Next we turn to King Saul, who is hiding from the Philistine army at Gilgal.[16] With his own soldiers deserting him and the immense Philistine force preparing an attack, Saul makes a decision from a place of doubt that will change his destiny. Having been instructed by God's prophet Samuel to wait for seven days – at which point Samuel will join the army at Gilgal to give a burnt offering to God – Saul gets cold feet and offers the sacrifice himself. It's the one thing he was specifically forbidden to do. You can imagine the scene as Samuel arrives to find the offering still smouldering. Saul knew what he was supposed to do, but as the situation he faced became increasingly pressured, along came doubt motivated by self-preservation.

'Did God *really* say you can't offer the sacrifice yourself?'

And the rest, as they say, is dynasty-destroying history.

Then we have Thomas. A young Jewish man who had given his life over to following a captivating, dynamic, wise and powerful rabbi called Jesus. A young man who had been willing to go to his death to follow his master. A young man who had come to believe that Jesus was the promised Messiah of Israel.[17] But now Thomas is a young man in despair and heartbreak. Jesus, his rabbi, his friend, his Messiah, was dead. As Thomas' friends tell him the amazing good news of the resurrection, a thought comes into his head.

'Did God *really* raise Jesus from the dead?'

And the rest, as they say, is nickname-producing history.

In each biblical story someone is confronted by doubt. Sometimes the question arises from our own misplaced desires. At other times the pressures of the world and our immediate circumstances prompt us. And we must be sober to the fact that Satan the accuser is still playing his same old tricks today. Make no mistake that Satan wants to steal your worship from God, and in doing so he also wants to steal your life, your hope and your identity. Satan's ultimate goal is to *dehumanise* you by pulling you away from the only foundation upon which human life can successfully be built – relationship with God. This is a big enough problem, but it gets worse because a dehumanised human always goes on to dehumanise other humans.

Dehumanisation is the rejection of empathy, the destruction of compassion, the superiority of self, the physical, emotional or spiritual killing of another. To dehumanise someone is to reject Jesus' standard of the so-called 'golden rule', of doing to others as you would have them do to you.[18] The philosopher Confucius had first articulated this truth almost five hundred years before Jesus, surely a reminder that it's fundamental to what it means to be human, to be beloved creations of God.

The Bible makes it clear that the ways we can dehumanise others are symptoms of the ultimate form of dehumanisation, rebellion against God. Rebellion against your creator literally steals away your humanity as you deny your true identity, and bring the catastrophic consequences of those actions to bear on the rest of humanity. Every time we reject God we dehumanise ourselves, and the dehumanisation of others in one way or another inevitably follows.

To truly be human is to be a worshipper of God in spirit and truth. The accuser knows what you were created for and he hates everything about it. He hates that your life should bring glory to God because he wants the glory for himself. And so the accuser will use one simple word to dehumanise you and make you a dehumaniser of others:

'Really?'

Satan is arrogant enough to assume that his use of this single word is more powerful than God's promises. All too frequently we let him be right.

But there is someone else in the Bible who faced the same question: the divine Son who took on flesh and became human in order to restore our relationship with our loving holy God. Jesus faced the direct accusation and temptation of Satan in the wilderness, but it is perhaps his retreat to pray in the garden of Gethsemane that, even though Satan is not explicitly mentioned in the narrative, best illustrates the point.[19] Jesus knows what must be done. It is a torturous and unbearable road ahead. He is in anguish. And somewhere in it all, a word is present.

'Really?'

When that question came, Adam and Eve let doubt prevail to enjoy more supposed freedom.

'Really?'

When that question came, Saul let doubt prevail to trust in his own power.

'Really?'

When that question came, Thomas let doubt prevail in favour of his emotions.

Jesus responds differently.

'Father if there is another way then let it be so, but not my will be done but yours.'

Unlike Adam and Eve, Jesus says to the Father, 'I find my freedom in you.' True freedom is found in submission to God, in trusting his perfect and good will even when it seems restrictive or costly. When the accuser asks you if you are really free, you can declare your foundation of freedom. You have been set free – 'free indeed' – and you will not return to the slavery of rebellion against God.[20]

Unlike Saul, Jesus says to the Father, 'The power is yours.' True power is not found in relying on our own strength or understanding, but in acknowledging that

God is sovereign. When the accuser questions if God is really powerful, if he'll really come through when you need him, you can declare your foundation of power. He who hung the stars in the sky is for you and not against you, his matchless power is at work in your life day by day and you have his spirit of power, love and self-discipline.[21]

Unlike Thomas, Jesus says to the Father, 'Not my emotion, but your promises.' Often we allow our circumstances to shake us from the promises of God. In the face of the suffering of the cross Jesus asks the Father to give him the perspective of heaven, to help him endure as his emotions conflict and confuse about the task ahead. When the accuser asks if God really cares about you, if he is really trustworthy, you can declare your foundation of promise. You can thank God that his plans formed long ago will be outworked with perfect faithfulness, for he is good and his loving kindness is everlasting, he is with you wherever you go and empowers you beyond your present understanding.[22]

Our response to the question of the accuser will determine whether we go on with our misunderstanding about what it means to be human or whether we accept God's promise to restore us to true life. Our response will be based on where we have built our foundation.

Jesus built his life on the perfect foundation of submission to, and trust in, the Father. While the questions still came and the struggle was real, he didn't fail to build his life upon that foundation in every circumstance, to seek first the kingdom and righteousness of his heavenly Father.[23] In the same way, we must build our own lives on the foundation of God's truth. Sometimes, though, we fall short and end up moving our foundations to places which seem to offer more security, pleasure, hope, comfort, or satisfaction.

My friend Joujou was showing me around the Egyptian capital Cairo on a recent visit, and he pointed out a number of collapsed buildings. I asked him why this was such a problem in the city, and his answer was simple.

'They are illegal buildings, put up quickly without the right regulations, and eventually they fall down – injuring and killing people.'

I asked Joujou why people moved into such buildings if they knew they were unsafe. He answered with sadness in his voice.

'Because it's all they can afford.'

How often do we choose the cheap route? How often do we break the building codes of God's law, racking up debts that we can't afford to pay and exposing ourselves to the inevitability of being crushed under the failure of our own construction? But even then, rather than leaving us buried under the rubble, God sent us the priceless treasure of heaven, his own Son, to pay our unpayable debt, to take upon himself the impact of the crushing weight of our collapse, and to show us what a life perfectly built upon God's foundation really looks like.

God's foundation of truth is the reality upon which we build our lives. God's forgiveness through Jesus is what saves it from crushing collapse.

When Peter hopped out of the boat to meet Jesus upon the waves he modelled perfectly how it looks to put your faith in Jesus. But the doubt that followed modelled perfectly how prone we are to sink and to be consumed by waves of circumstance as we lose sight of Jesus and begin to mistrust the foundation he offers us.

In his grace Jesus lifts us up again and again from the waves, rescuing us from our frailty. And as he does so, Jesus also asks us again and again, 'Why do you have so little faith that leads to doubt?' His compassionate question is not there to bring shame, but to call us into a better way of living, to the full adventure and freedom of really trusting him.

Jesus doesn't shame or condemn Thomas for his doubt. He simply invites his disciple to move beyond misunderstanding and explore truth for himself: 'Come here if you need to, Thomas, place your fingers in my wounds, investigate me and realise this is reality.'

The gesture is staggeringly gracious, offering the hope of rescue from debilitating doubt. Likewise, this is the way we are to meet people in their doubt today, with mercy, and the loving invitation to explore Jesus for themselves.[24]

Does Thomas take Jesus up on his offer? The great Italian painter Caravaggio thought so, as we see in his stunning work *The Incredulity of Saint Thomas*. Caravaggio shows Thomas touching Jesus' wounds as Peter and John watch closely to satisfy their own curiosity. It's a captivating image.

But as beautiful as the painting is, it's also entirely speculative. John doesn't tell us whether Thomas actually touched Jesus' scars. That's not the point of the story. What John is showing us is that Jesus doesn't confront doubt with condemnation, but invitation.

Jesus invites each of us to come and investigate his life for ourselves, to taste and see that he is good, to bring the weariness of our existence to him and know rest and hope in his peace.[25] Some see miraculous signs, others have to make do with the testimony of the apostles, and the ongoing testimony of believers today.[26] Thomas had the privilege of seeing the resurrected Jesus with his own eyes, but Jesus says the rest of us are more blessed if we are able to trust in him having not seen. Why would this be so? Because faith is what pleases God, and it takes greater faith to trust in something you have not seen.

To build your life on the foundation of God's truth by trusting in Jesus is the ultimate form of worship and what brings the greatest blessing. To do the opposite brings the greatest failure, and ultimately leads to death. But failure doesn't need to be final with God.

Satan had never met a human he couldn't lead into sin-inducing doubt, that he couldn't dehumanise, until he met the incarnate Jesus. While we were still sinners building our lives on faulty foundations, the perfectly human Jesus died for us.[27] It was forgiveness, not a curse, that Jesus spoke over his enemies from the cross. It was compassion that poured from his lips, not condemnation.[28] In his resurrection Jesus demonstrated that God is the life-giving, hope-securing foundation of true humanity. Through his life, death and resurrection, Jesus offers all those whose lives are built on the faulty foundations of rebellion against God a way to the solid foundation of the Father.[29]

The victorious risen Jesus invites each of us to stop doubting and believe. It's an invitation to confident hope – a hope that will not put us to shame.[30] As Ravi Zacharias powerfully expresses, this invitation provokes a greater shock than even the most overwhelming circumstances of life or the most confrontational accusations of Satan:

> Our biggest shock is coming face-to-face with God and discovering that he comes, not merely offering us forgiveness, but that he knows who we really are and still offers us forgiveness. He knows our debt, and he alone has the resources to cover it. This is the story of grace beyond our understanding.[31]

God could legitimately give each of us a condemning nickname. Sinful Ben. Rebellious Kate. Doubting Thomas. The list could go on and on. But these are not the names he gives us. Doubting Thomas is not the name by which Jesus knew his friend, even though he knew his doubt. Instead, Jesus met Thomas in his moment of struggle and made the way for him, and for each of us, to receive the name by which we can now be called. That all who trust in his name are given the right to be called children of God.[32]

The world watches on as the accuser asks, 'Is Jesus *really* your resurrected Lord?' Our answer defies his dehumanising schemes and empowers us to walk through the overwhelming circumstances of life. Our answer lets the world know that there is hope, as we reply with our lips and our lives, 'He is my Lord and my God.'

ONE: DOUBTING

CHAPTER ONE: DISCUSSION QUESTIONS

How do we best approach doubt as followers of Jesus?

What foundations do people build their lives upon?

How can we respond to the doubt-inducing accusations of the enemy?

How might we help someone journey through their doubts about faith in Jesus?

CHAPTER ONE: APPLICATION

Explore running something like an Alpha or Christianity Explored course through your church. These courses are a great way to allow people to ask questions, share their doubts about faith and learn what Christianity is all about, and a great first step into basic evangelism for many people. Find out more at **alpha.org** and **christianityexplored.org**.

TWO
ISOLATED

Now Thomas (also known as Didymus), one of the Twelve, was not with the disciples when Jesus came.
JOHN 20:24

It's curious that Thomas is not with the other disciples when Jesus first appears to them after his resurrection. The Bible doesn't tell us why. We could guess – maybe Thomas was in the middle of a mistimed Starbucks run? Or, less anachronistically, we might reasonably wonder if Thomas was away from his friends because of his grief.[33]

Have you ever experienced something so painful that you just wanted to be alone? After another heart-breaking football World Cup exit by the English national men's team I remember a friend of mine being so distraught that he had to take himself into another room to sit on his own and mourn. His girlfriend couldn't make sense of why he was so upset or why he wanted to be left alone at such a time, and the relationship never really recovered from the argument that followed. Losing the World Cup dream and a girlfriend in the same day is enough for anyone to start channelling their inner Greta Garbo.[34]

Fair enough, this seems a little trivial in comparison with someone needing to isolate themselves because of a bereavement. But it is a good example of how, whether you're facing life's big or seemingly small challenges, sometimes you just need a bit of space.

There's a big difference between isolation and solitude. Sometimes we might need to find solitude in order to create space for reflection or even to escape distraction as we attempt to complete a task. In John Mark Comer's helpful book *The Ruthless Elimination of Hurry* he draws the distinction:

> Solitude is engagement; isolation is escape. Solitude is safety; isolation is danger. Solitude is how you open yourself up to God; isolation is painting a target on your back for the tempter. Solitude is when you set aside time to feed and water and nourish your soul. To let it grow into health and maturity. Isolation is what you crave when you neglect the former. And solitude – as somber as it sounds – is anything but loneliness.[35]

The very idea of intentional solitude is actually key to the Christian discipleship journey. In the gospels, Jesus himself regularly retreats to places of solitude to pray, reflect, listen, refresh and worship the Father. It's a practice that we don't tend to be so good at today in our busy and ever-connected online lives, to the detriment of our walk with Jesus and all the health benefits – spiritual, physical, mental and emotional – that come along with it. But the problem our world faces isn't that we're spending too much time in solitude, or intentional aloneness. The problem our world faces is that we're spending too much time in isolation.

As I'm writing these words, the world is in the grip of the Covid-19 pandemic, with countries around the globe employing social isolation techniques to stem the spread of the virus. Isolation in this case serves a positive purpose, but as a pragmatic solution rather than an end in itself. No one wants our present enforced isolation to become a permanent reality and, while the isolation will help slow the spread of the virus, the mental health implications of isolation are going to be challenging for many.

It should be no surprise to us that isolation is used as a technique to deal with bad behaviour in many prisons around the world, or as a form of torture for those in captivity. The stories of those who have experienced long-term isolation and its effects make for particularly harrowing reading.[36] Isolation doesn't just impact a person emotionally, it can actually cause your brain to rewire itself in detrimental ways and it leads to decreased motivation and attention to taking good physical care of yourself.

TWO: ISOLATED

When kidnapped humanitarian Terry Waite was finally moved into a cell with three other men after four years of isolation, he wasn't sure that he still knew how to communicate with another person. As he listened to the stories of one of his cell mates, he realised that this new companion was using the memories of relational connection to 'hold on to his identity and convince himself that he had a life and was and is a person of worth.'[37] Isolation can result in the stripping away of our identity and our value.

An obvious emotional side effect of isolation is loneliness. Psychologists assert that long-term loneliness is one of the most destructive mental states a person can experience.[38] Loneliness and isolation are not the same thing, but one can lead to the other. Yet, while it is likely that those who experience isolation will feel lonely, not all who are lonely are necessarily alone.

Just as there is a difference between solitude and isolation, so there is between aloneness and loneliness. In his brilliant book *Together*, former US Surgeon General Vivek Murthy describes loneliness as:

> ...the subjective feeling that you're lacking the social connections you need. It can feel like being stranded, abandoned, or cut off from the people with whom you belong – even if you're surrounded by other people. What's missing when you're lonely is the feeling of closeness, trust, and the affection of genuine friends, loved ones, and community...

> While loneliness engenders despair and ever more isolation, togetherness raises optimism and creativity. When people feel they belong to one another, their lives are stronger, richer, and more joyful.[39]

Loneliness is a complicated emotional state, often bringing with it feelings of shame, embarrassment, inadequacy, and hopelessness. Those who experience loneliness – even while surrounded by others – are often likely to end up isolating themselves in the long term.

Isn't it deeply troubling that, despite having more methods of communication and social interaction than ever before, we as a society are becoming more isolated than connected, and more lonely than relationally fulfilled?[40]

If long-term loneliness is a negative experience that needs attention and correction, the actual feeling of being lonely is your brain's way of telling you that you need connection.[41] It's almost as if the chemistry of our brains inherently knows that we were not made to be on our own. Those feelings of loneliness are a reminder that we were created for connection with God. They point us back to our primary connection, our primary source of trust, affection and community. Pointing us back to God, the ultimate source of relational community.

Have you ever stopped to reflect on the fact that you were created from an eternal relationship? That might sound confusing, but remember the most distinctive

Christian claim about God. He is triune – an eternal undivided unity expressed in three persons – Father, Son, and Holy Spirit.[42]

I've lost count of the number of times people have asked me if God created us because he was bored and lonely. Erm, no. God has never been alone, he has always been in perfect relationship with himself, the three persons of the Trinity in glorious loving union for all eternity. It is from this perfect relationship that God creates us for perfect relationship.

At the risk of perpetuating multiple heresies about the nature of the Trinity and the concept of eternity (these are the things that keep me up at night), it's almost as if Father, Son and Spirit looked at each other in the same eternal moment and experienced a perfect desire to share their perfect relationship with a creation. God didn't create us because he was lonely, he created us because he was perfectly fulfilled. And here we are, able to share in that perfect fulfilment.

To paraphrase Francis Bacon, the worst isolation is the lack of true relationship.[43] Time and again we choose loneliness by isolating ourselves from God, our ultimate source of true relationship, fulfilment, and love. As we isolate ourselves from our creator, loneliness grips and we seek to find fulfilment in something, anything, that fills the void. The results are shockingly destructive. But despite our rejection, God by his grace makes a way for us to know physical, emotional and spiritual wholeness once more.

I'm pretty much slap-bang in the middle of the introvert or extrovert scale. That means that there are times when I'm happy to be the life and soul of the party, and also times when I need my own space. But this doesn't really come down to personality types. Each of us also has a need to be with others that transcends our personality type.

For example, you might be the most introverted person in the world, but if you fall into a hole with no one around to help, you'll soon be making as much noise as the most extroverted person around (or unfortunately for you, not around). As the Bible tells us, 'Two are better than one, because they have a good return for their labour: If either of them falls down, one can help the other up.'[44]

We can all think of a time when we needed someone to help us in a practical way, but that's hardly getting to the nitty-gritty of our problem of isolation and loneliness. It can be hard to make yourself emotionally vulnerable to others, but I suspect that Solomon had emotional and spiritual needs in mind just as much as physical needs as he wrote those words from Ecclesiastes.

The more we become physically, emotionally and spiritually isolated from those who can look out for us, encourage and affirm us, and hold us to account for the way we are living, the more likely we are to lose our way, not least in our walk with God. We can hide behind personality types all day long ('I just need my own space') but even those who need more time alone than others still need connection with God as their primary source at all times and supportive connection with others along the way too.

German theologian Dietrich Bonhoeffer warns that, 'Sin wants to be alone with people. It takes them away from the community. The more lonely people become, the more destructive the power of sin over them.'[45] It is when we are alone that we are most vulnerable to temptation.

Not only do we find accountability in community to help us avoid sin, but we also find forgiveness when we fall short. Sometimes the best way for us to realise there is something in our lives that needs correction is when someone else points it out to us.[46] And we find that God has given us the power to correct the sin in our lives – the good Father has acted through his Son to make forgiveness possible, and he prompts us and empowers us by his Spirit to repent, to change direction.

As we turn from our isolation from our heavenly Father and commit to the community of God and his people, we begin to see change in our lives. We find that we are fulfilled in a way that we didn't previously realise was possible. Our loneliness can be replaced with holiness.

God calls us to be a holy people. God shows us what holiness truly is, and in the community of the church we help one another to grow in that same holiness. Each of us is responsible for our own lives, but each of us is called to help each other as members of one family. Holiness is an individual responsibility best worked out as a shared pursuit.

Privacy and individualism are relatively new ways of living. In Jesus' world, privacy was a luxury reserved for the wealthy. Most lived openly among their neighbours and people knew one another's business for good or ill.[47] Our quest for individualism and privacy has taken us down an unexpected road of loneliness, isolation and despair. We thought privacy and individualism would lead to greater freedom to be our true selves, to pursue greater fulfilment and satisfaction on our own terms, but we ended up privatising our own lives and creating an idol of individuality. We forgot what we were designed for.

God's way is relationship. Connection. God's way is service and sacrifice. God's way is other before self. God's way is for us to be together in this world as we prepare to be together with him eternally in the next. Even when it's annoying and messy. In fact, especially when it's annoying and messy.

Sadly, our churches, which were once a place for our daily Christian lives to be exposed to the needs of the wider community, often now function as a weekly get-together before we 'go back to our lives.' The early church didn't have lives to go back to, they were the church, the hope of the world, present with God, taking care of each other, available to the world that it might, by trust in Jesus Christ, become the church too.

As Christians our lives are now inseparably bound up in the community of God and his people. The concern of the kingdom becomes our own. God sent his Son to save the world from isolating itself against him and the horrendous immediate and eternal consequences that follow. Now he sends his people to go in Jesus' name to rescue those who are still in isolation from him. The church is the antidote to loneliness in the world, not because we give people a place to come and meet others once or twice a week, but because we carry the power of connection to the source of eternal relationship in our words and our deeds.

According to Hollywood legend Orson Welles, 'We're born alone, we live alone, we die alone. Only through our love and friendship can we create the illusion for the moment that we're not alone.'[48] If this is true, the best we can hope for is to fool and distract ourselves from the painful reality of being alone. The church cannot simply be another distraction from reality, but must be the living revelation of the truth that ushers in the hope of a new reality of togetherness for all – the gospel.

My friend MK grew up in a fatherless home in the impoverished Cape Town township of Gugulethu. His challenging upbringing was a one-way ticket to gangsterism for a young boy like MK. Looking for acceptance, community and status, it wasn't long until he was prowling the streets of the nearby Nyanga township – the so-called 'murder capital' of South Africa and one of the most dangerous places to live in the world – as he rose through the ranks of his gang to become a major player. Eventually the consequences of gangsterism caught up with him and an eighteen-year prison sentence followed. In the early days of prison, hardly a day passed where MK didn't have either his own or someone else's blood on his hands. MK's life was the definition of disconnection and the consequences were horrendously destructive.

One day MK was given a copy of Rick Warren's *The Purpose Driven Life* and began to read it. In its pages he discovered the profound biblical truth that he was not an accident in this universe. His life has purpose and meaning given to him by his creator who has made it possible to be reconnected with and adopted into the family of God. MK gave his life to Jesus in prison.

Now released, MK is living again today in the township of Nyanga where he plays an active role in offering a better community to boys at risk of falling into gangsterism – a community of hope and life through fellowship with God and his people the church. MK could have chosen to live somewhere else – somewhere safer – but he knows that God has saved him from the destructive path of isolation at the cost of his own Son. For MK, isolating himself from those who need the love and fellowship of Christ the most, whatever the personal cost, would be to live again in selfish isolation.

God calls his people to reject living in isolation from him and to embrace fellowship with him. He calls his people to reject living in isolation from the needs of the world and embrace fellowship with the world for him.

It's painful at times, but it leads to joy. It's messy, but it leads to beauty. It's costly, but it's truly rewarding. And God is with us in it all.

The Bible declares that God knew us even before we were knitted together in our mother's womb.[49] The gospel reveals the reality of the God who came to be with us when we had run away from him.[50] The Bible assures us that no one needs to die alone, for by Jesus' death and resurrection we are no longer subject to the full, lonely, eternally-isolating sting of death. Instead, those who trust in Jesus as Lord will draw a final breath in this life as we take our first breath in the next. God walks us through the mere shadow of death and into the fullness of the new life that awaits. Perfect, eternal communion with God and his children.

God does not abandon us in the life that we live until that moment comes. Yes, there will be followers of Jesus who experience loneliness in this life, even though they know him. Our world is not yet restored to the full glory that awaits when Jesus returns, and Christians are not immune to difficulty and pain. But as we encounter complicated emotions and circumstances in this life, the eternal God of relationship makes available to us his perfect love every day, and works on our behalf to draw us into an ever deeper relationship with him.

To satisfy our human need for connection we look to our primary source himself, our loving God. It is a connection that is deepened by fellowship with other believers, the Christ community we call the church, the family of God. It is a connection that at times can feel distant, confusing, and less than what God has promised. But it is a connection that will not lead to disappointment as we grow in our trust of him until the day we see him face to face. The day when we will never know loneliness again.

We can't know for sure why Thomas wasn't with his friends when Jesus appeared. But we do know that when they came calling, despite his doubt and grief, he was reconnected with community when the resurrected Jesus appeared to them a second time, and he was never the same again.

And so we as the church go to an isolated and lonely world with the best news of all time:

Haven't you heard? You are not alone. He is risen.

TWO: ISOLATED

CHAPTER TWO: DISCUSSION QUESTIONS

Do you struggle more with committing to connection with others or intentional solitude?

What does the word community mean to you?

How can we as the church respond to the loneliness of the world?

Why is the resurrection of Christ the ultimate answer to loneliness?

CHAPTER TWO: APPLICATION

Think about the people who live on your street or in your immediate neighbourhood. What would it look like for you to create a sense of genuine community with those who live closest to you? In the meeting of practical need and the gentle but clear offering of spiritual support (like prayer) you may transform someone's daily existence, and expose them to the hope of full life in Jesus.

THREE
BROKEN

But he said to them, 'Unless I see the nail marks in
his hands and put my finger where the nails were,
and put my hand into his side, I will not believe.'
JOHN 20:25

One Christmas morning many years ago marked a rare occasion in my life. I was speechless. My parents had saved all year to buy me my very own desktop computer, something I had desperately wanted for months. Never in a million years did I expect to receive such an expensive gift that Christmas.[51]

The size of the present made me curious as soon as I saw it, but even as I ripped off the wrapping paper and exposed the clear branding and product details on the box I couldn't quite take it all in. Was I dreaming? Was this a cruel joke (no doubt orchestrated by my sister)? Surely this was too good to be reality...

THREE: BROKEN

There are times in our lives when we are told things that just seem too good to be true. It's one thing for us to go to the world with the good news, another thing entirely for the world to receive it.

When Thomas hears his friends announce the news of Jesus' resurrection, we might expect him to jump up, shout 'Hallelujah!' and go running to find his risen Messiah. But instead, he looks at them and says, 'On your bike, lads.'

It's no stretch to assume that Thomas would have wanted Jesus' resurrection to be true more than anything, so why didn't he trust his friends when they came with the good news? This was no group of strangers trying to con him. He knew these men, he knew that they too had been grieving. If this was a prank, it was staggeringly insensitive. So perhaps Thomas could believe their sincerity, but dismissed it as wishful thinking. They must have just seen someone who looked like Jesus.

Have you ever been away from someone you care about for so long that you keep thinking you see them in people who look vaguely similar? Deep down you know it can't be them, but there's just enough of a familiarity in someone's appearance, walk, voice or presence that tricks you for a moment. Hope can be a powerful force in expanding your perception. Then again, grief can be an equally powerful force in stunting your perception of reality. As C.S. Lewis wrote of his own grief, 'You can't see anything properly while your eyes are blurred with tears.'[52]

Earlier I mentioned Caravaggio's *The Incredulity of Saint Thomas*. I think incredulity is a helpful way of looking at it. To be incredulous is to be unwilling or unable to believe something. When faced with Thomas' doubt many assume he was sceptical, stubbornly unwilling to believe in this extraordinary and implausible event. But don't forget that Thomas had seen Lazarus raised from the dead. Perhaps he wasn't sceptical, but simply unable to believe the claim of resurrection because of his grief.[53]

Doesn't it make sense for Thomas to be so heartbroken by the death of Jesus that he couldn't let himself believe the resurrection was true in case it turned out not to be? Sometimes hope is too painful a burden to carry. If hope turns out to be false then the healing process takes longer. Sometimes it's easier to ignore hope and commit to the difficult road of acceptance that moves a person towards recovery from trauma and grief.[54]

What Thomas needed to shake him from his grief was not the mere hope of the resurrection, but the reality of it. And so in his grief Thomas rejects the claims of his friends and sets the criteria that he will need to believe. He needs nothing less than the empirical proof of the risen Jesus' wounded body for inspection. For Thomas, hope is too risky.

We live in a sceptical world. In our post-enlightenment, science-obsessed (worshipping?) and often-fickle culture, the claims of the Christian faith are more likely to be met with mockery than intrigue. But the need to see it before we believe it is nothing new. It's not even new to John's gospel by the time Thomas states his own empirical needs. Long before that moment Jesus had already revealed his frustration with those who were too reliant on visible evidence.[55]

The world is broken by sin and that includes our ability to perceive things correctly. Faith itself is often perceived in negative terms as a crutch for the weak or stupid, and a problem of integrity for the strong or intelligent who should know better. But the biblical picture of faith is 'confidence in what we hope for and assurance about what we do not see.'[56] Faith in God as revealed through his word gives us the opportunity to correct our faulty perspective. Those who trust in the steadfastness and righteousness of God will themselves be made steadfast and righteous. They will be restored, healed and made whole. We are not called to blind faith – there is hard evidence in the frame – but it is faith, nonetheless.[57]

Once, after a speaking engagement at a university in the UK, I found myself in an extended conversation with the head of the local humanist society. During the Q&A time he had presented and argued for his sceptical viewpoints with confidence and thoughtfulness. But now we were talking more personally, away from the eyes and ears of those in attendance and away from formality and the need to present 'answers'. Now it was just two blokes in friendly conversation, and as we talked he began to open up about his life. He had grown up in a Christian home, with a religiously strict and dogmatic father, and lots of experience of unanswered prayer. I'm not saying that these things are explicitly what led him to his scepticism (people are more complicated than that) but it struck an interesting chord all the same.

As we finished up, I asked him if he would like me to pray for him and he paused for a moment before saying no. I asked if he was sure – after all, what did he have to lose? His answer took me a little by surprise. He said that he didn't want me to pray because part of him would want the prayer to be answered and he couldn't allow himself to believe that could happen. He didn't want the hope of an answered prayer for fear of it being unfounded. His scepticism was a more comfortable foundation for him than the risk of taking a step of faith towards Jesus.

Later that evening the event organiser sent me a message saying that the humanist had thanked him for putting the event on and had said the following words as he left: 'That young man has given me a lot to think about.'

As I've already said, the act of proclaiming the good news and people receiving it are two different things. There are so many reasons why people can't or won't put their trust in Jesus. It's rarely (if ever) as simple as saying, 'Look, you're just being sceptical and you need to get over your stubbornness and have some faith already!' Rather than dismissing an unbelieving world, and even though – like Jesus – we might be exasperated at times, through patience, love, and attention to need, over time we might move a person just a little closer to the reality of the cross. After all, how much patience does the Lord show us each day as we journey in relationship with him?

The power of salvation belongs to God alone, but the pathway to his love is paved with the lives of his people who take the brokenness of the lost seriously. People who, figuratively at least, lay down their lives upon the rocky and painful road to the cross that they might make the journey more accessible for an unbelieving and conflicted world to walk towards Jesus. There will be those who stay committed to other idols and remain sceptical no matter what we do, but our commitment is to keep reaching out to them, and, whatever the reason for their rejection, scepticism, or unbelief, to keep revealing Jesus as the answer in word and deed.

Jesus literally laid down his life in the ultimate expression of relationship-restoring sacrificial love, but after his resurrection he also distinctively met his disciples in their individual trust issues and helped them move beyond them. Biblical scholar Grant Osborne points out:

Mary needed the voice of the Good Shepherd; the disciples needed to see Jesus' wounds and know it was truly him; Thomas needs to touch those self-same wounds. Jesus meets those needs right where they are and turns [lives] around.[58]

God will not force his way into the heart of the sceptic or anyone else unless there is an opening of their own will. As sceptical as Thomas appeared to be, Jesus knew the real reason why he was struggling to believe. Jesus sees beneath the surface, through the outward appearance to the real issue.[59] By his grace he saw through Thomas' demand for empirical verification and gave him something better: an encounter.

We use all sorts of words to greet people. Some are formal and some are intimate, some make an enquiry about a person's wellbeing, and others relate to the time of day. John tells us that the risen Jesus greeted his assembled disciples by saying, 'Peace be with you.' Such a greeting would have been familiar to these Jewish men, especially when expressed in the form of the Hebrew word *shalom*.[60]

Ask anyone vaguely familiar with the word *shalom* about its meaning, and they are likely to summarise it as 'peace.' Broadly speaking this is correct, but a fuller explanation would be something along the lines of: 'Nothing is broken, nothing is missing, all is as it should be.'[61] To quote Bruce Milne, '*shalom* is life at its best under the gracious hand of God.'[62]

And yet, look around you. Does the world look like nothing is broken or missing? Which is the better description: peace or chaos? Some might point to the fact that we are enjoying a period of sustained peace from war (among the global superpowers at least) so far this century.[63] But then we are forced to confront staggeringly poor mental health, shockingly high suicide rates, a global pandemic, the appalling effects of racism, the prevalence of school shootings (particularly in the US), the destructiveness of addiction – from substance abuse to gambling – and the list goes on and on.

One of my favourite films is the war epic *The Thin Red Line*. Unlike many Hollywood depictions of war, filmmaker Terence Malick is more interested in the impact of suffering in the world than heroism and battle scenes. Malick's film has a simple but deeply profound conclusion – that suffering causes separation. Writing about the film, scholar Michael Chion comes to this striking revelation:

> In the man who sees another suffering, it creates a feeling of almost total powerlessness to lessen that suffering, and in the one who is suffering, a symmetrical sense of powerlessness to speak of his suffering or to share it. The paradox of the human condition is that we all suffer without distinction...and the thing that makes us all fellows in our fate is also the thing that drives us apart as we experience it.[64]

We all experience suffering. Tragically, it's one of the things that unifies our human experience. And yet even though it unifies us, it doesn't unite us. It separates us. Suffering is liable to lead us into more doubt, more isolation, and more brokenness. It was the separation of humanity from God by our sin that led to suffering in the world, and it is that very same suffering that separates us from the rest of creation.

In reflecting on his experience of attempting to relate to the suffering of those closest to him, C. S. Lewis melancholically observed that, 'You can't really share someone else's weakness, or fear or pain. What you feel may be bad. It might conceivably be as bad as what the other felt... But it would still be quite different.'[65]

Even when our suffering seems comparable, we can never truly share the experience of another person. Even if we have great capacity for empathy, there is always distance at play, always some level of separation. But there is one exception to this troubling reality. Jesus.

In her wonderful book on evangelism, *Stay Salt*, Becky Pippert shares this thought:

> In all of the religions of the world, it is only the Christian God who bears scars. With all the suffering in our world, it would be hard to trust a God who had not suffered. But Jesus has suffered, and he didn't have to; he chose to! His scars reveal that he understands the difficulties of life far better than we do. He's been here. He knows.[66]

It gets better still. The full reality of Jesus' suffering goes further than a deeper empathy with us. Jesus suffered uniquely by taking the sin and chaos of the world upon himself, so that we might be brought to forgiveness, righteousness and peace.[67] Jesus knows exactly what it is like for you to suffer, not because he's known suffering similar to yours, but because he has worn the pain of your actual sufferings in wearing the weight of your sin upon the cross.

Just when it looked like chaos was winning, when *shalom* had become only an ironic greeting, up stepped Jesus to overcome the chaos and win the ultimate victory of peace. Wholeness replaced brokenness. Light replaced darkness. Life replaced death.

As the risen Jesus appears before his disciples this common greeting carries its full meaning at last, as R. C. Sproul explains:

> Before his death, he promised the full reality of the bequest of his peace on these people. Now, having been raised from the dead, he entered their midst and said, 'Peace be with you.' Then he showed them his hands and his side, as if to say, 'I did what I said I was going to do, and I have won that peace for you.'[68]

While human suffering separates, the suffering of Christ eternally unites us to him, and as we live for him, it unites us to the needs of the world. We can't know each person's suffering as they do, but Jesus does, and so we go compassionately to the world in and through him.

Thomas may have been guilty of being slow on a few areas of Jesus' teaching, but one thing he couldn't have failed to recognise was his rabbi's obsession with the kingdom of God.

The kingdom is wrapped up in a dual reality – both present now in the form of God at work in and through his people in our imperfect and temporary world, and with its full reality yet to come when the imperfection and finiteness of this world comes to an end, and the perfection of heaven takes hold forevermore.[69] The victory of the cross has made wholeness, healing and peace with God possible. One day it will be perfectly so, as heaven breaks into our reality. But until then, it is the Spirit-empowered people of God who are to be the living embodiment of *shalom* in our chaotic world, bringing the power and peace of heaven to earth today as we reveal the authenticity of his *shalom*-securing resurrection.

How do you imagine heaven? Some picture it as a cartoon-like sky realm where we all have our own cloud and hope that our closest cloud neighbour plays the harp better than we do. For others, it's the image of a restored Eden, the perfect garden where God, man and nature are in unbroken harmonious relationship, which surely includes pet kangaroos for all. Others imagine the gold-paved streets of the new Jerusalem while wondering if we'll have suitable heavenly footwear to avoid either slipping on or scuffing up the shiny surfaces.

We can get easily side-tracked on questions about what heaven will look like, where it is, or whether we'll mainly be singing hymns or the latest Hillsong hits for the next ten thousand years, and end up missing the point. God wants to assure us of the reality and character of the kingdom of heaven, its king, and the present and eternal hope of restored relationship with him.

Heaven is indeed a place, and a place where God himself resides and rules to the perfect standard and outworking of his equally perfect will.[70] It's where Jesus came from, where he has gone to prepare a place for us, and the place from where he will return at the end of days when we will be with and worship him eternally.[71] And yes, throughout scripture we are given tantalising glimpses of what heaven will be like. But we best encounter the idea of heaven in relation to its essential character, not its aesthetics.[72] The Bible reveals that the kingdom of heaven is everlasting, righteous and joyful, full of love, peace, kindness and goodness.[73] The descriptions go on, but we can sum it up in a word:

Shalom.

It would be easy to think that the greatest benefit of heaven is eternal life, but no, the Bible affirms that the greatest reward of heaven is actually Jesus himself. The eternal hope that awaits those who trust in Jesus is to be with and worship the Prince of Peace forever.

The intersection of heaven and earth is Jesus. He is the reality of the gospel's eternal power and peace taking hold of our finite and broken human lives.[74] Our credentials to be ambassadors of heaven are nothing more or less than the saving power of the gospel itself, its truth revealed in the transformation of our lives as we trust in Jesus as Lord. Our actions as ambassadors in our world are not self-motivated, self-empowered acts of kindness for arbitrary 'positive' impact, but daily, worship-motivated, Spirit-empowered acts of announcement to our perfect king that, 'Your will be done in and through my life and on this earth, as it is eternally in my true home of heaven,' and announce to the world that there is hope – even in our greatest struggles and pain.

We may not always have perfect answers to why suffering or calamity takes place, but we can as the people of God offer an answer to the effects of suffering and calamity as we trust that Jesus will one day separate us from the presence of pain and chaos. You may be wondering why God doesn't just send a quick fix now, a thunderbolt in our time of need, but as Tom Wright explains:

God does send thunderbolts – human ones. He sends in the poor in spirit, the meek, the mourners, the peacemakers, the hungry-for-justice people. They are the way God wants to act in his world. They are more effective than any lightning flashes or actual thunderbolts. They will use their initiative; they will see where the real needs are, and go to meet them. They will weep at the tombs of their friends. At the tombs of their enemies. Some of them will get hurt. Some may be killed. That is the story of Acts, all through. There will be problems, punishments, setbacks, shipwrecks, but God's purpose will come through. These people, prayerful, humble, faithful, will be the answer, not to the question Why? But to the question What? What needs to be done here? Who is most at risk? How can we help? Who shall we send? God works in all things with and through those who love him.[75]

Like Thomas before us, as we encounter the risen Jesus we can begin to move on from our scepticism and realise by the scars of his suffering that he is trustworthy.

We become life-givers where we once only dealt in death, united with God through his rescue plan of the gospel. We become peacemakers where we were once chaos-bringers, united with each other in fellowship with Christ. We become hope-carriers where we once only knew brokenness, united with the Spirit to face the sufferings of the world with the gospel of peace in word and deed.

Thomas may have had the benefit of seeing the risen Jesus with his own eyes, but you have the greater blessing of encountering the risen Jesus in daily steps of God-pleasing, perspective-setting, course-correcting, peace-bringing, life-giving faith.

This good news isn't too good to be true. It's just too good to be anything other than Jesus.

CHAPTER THREE: DISCUSSION QUESTIONS

What about Christianity might seem too good to be true for those we know?

In what ways might people need their perspective shifting on the road to Jesus?

How do we live out the peace of Christ in our world today?

How might we reveal that hope in Jesus is a risk worth taking?

CHAPTER THREE: APPLICATION

Pray daily for the *shalom* peace of God to be evident in your life and present in your relationships. Ask God for opportunities for you to be a peacemaker in your street, office, school, home, and wherever you go. Be prepared for this daily prayer to be answered with opportunities to reveal Jesus' peace and grace to those around you in often surprising ways.

PART TWO
THE DISCIPLE

FOUR
WORSHIPPER

Thomas said to him, 'My Lord and my God!'
JOHN 20:28

I'm a big fan of film music. While writing much of this book I've been accompanied by my friends Zimmer, Williams, Barry, Newman, and many other great composers. But as much as I enjoy cranking up the volume on a rousing film score at home while I write, it doesn't come close to the experience of being sat in a concert venue like the Royal Albert Hall in London and hearing a full orchestra build to the climactic crescendo of your favourite piece while surrounded by others all sharing in the same wonderful experience.

In John's gospel, the apostle writes as a conductor moving his baton to the opening notes of a symphony. In the very first moments of his gospel, the seeds of the crescendo to come are established:

'In the beginning was the Word, and the Word was with God, and the Word was God.'

Another flick of the baton.

'No one has ever seen God, but the one and only Son, who is himself God and is in closest relationship with the Father, has made him known.'

Now we move beyond the opening notes and into the first movement of the symphony. The conductor leads us through its developments, the content both mystifyingly complex and profoundly simple.

'I Am…'

Then, just as the symphony threatens to overwhelm – as John leads us through the pain and beauty of the cross – he surprises us with another turn of the baton and we are led into the awe and wonder of the resurrection. The conductor confidently moves from one movement to another, excitedly preparing to bring his audience to the climax that lies ahead.[76] The crescendo is in sight. It has all been building to this. With one final twist of the baton, the conductor unleashes the full weight of the climax upon his mesmerised audience…

FOUR: WORSHIPPER

'My Lord...'

Intensifying...

'...and my...'

Crescendo...

'...God.'

These five words uttered in a small room in Jerusalem in the presence of a dozen or so others are more awe-inspiring, beautiful, profound and moving than anything in all the works of the great composers or anything performed in the most magnificent of music venues to the greatest of crowds. These five words are the eternity-defining worship of Jesus Christ as the living God.

You probably know someone who doesn't always think before speaking. That person who at some point during a dinner party will say something that causes every jaw in the room to react as if they've only just discovered the effects of gravity.

As we will see in the final two chapters of this book, Thomas is not unaccustomed to opening his mouth, even when it puts others in a potentially awkward spot. But, save for Jesus' own teaching, nothing quite compares to Thomas' proclamation here when it comes to jaw-to-the-floor statements. Was it just a slip of the tongue? A shock-prompted profanity? A misunderstanding?

Jesus had been rightly recognised in some capacity as Messiah on a couple of occasions during his ministry, not least by the disciples, but this is the first occasion on which someone looks Jesus in the face and directly calls him God. In the moment that Thomas was confronted with the risen Jesus, there were many things that he could have proclaimed. John's gospel has already been full of pronouncements from others about Jesus.[77] Thomas could have shouted 'Teacher' (*rabboni*) as Mary did in the tomb garden when she realised who the 'gardener' was, 'Son of God' as John the Baptist testified, 'King' as Nathanael had confessed, 'Messiah' as Martha had confessed, or 'Saviour' as a group of Samaritans had marvelled.

But Thomas instinctively used the word 'Lord' followed by the word 'God'.

The word for 'Lord' used here (*kyrios*) is the same word used in the Greek translation of the Old Testament for YHWH, God's high name.[78] But the Greek word for Lord is also used in a variety of ways in the New Testament and most commonly means 'sir' or at times with higher intention, 'master'.

But here 'Lord' is followed by 'God' (*theos*). As those two words combine to form Thomas' proclamation towards Jesus, he verbally catches up with the heavenly realm in which the twenty-four eternal elders fall in worship before the throne of God, forever proclaiming, 'You are worthy, our Lord and God, to receive glory and honour and power, for you created all things, and by your will they were created and have their being.'[79]

Others throughout history have tried to make claim to the same identity that Thomas bestows upon Jesus. The Roman emperor Domitian (81–96 AD) demanded to be called 'Lord and God' (*Dominus et Deus*) by his subjects and became one of the most aggressive persecutors of Christians, no doubt in part because of the allegiance of Christ followers to Jesus, their true Lord and God.[80] But while pretenders to the heavenly throne are reduced to demanding their subjects call and worship them as such, relying on tyrannical behaviour to sustain the lie, the proclamation from Thomas' mouth was entirely voluntary.

Jesus makes no verbal demand of Thomas that he must be acknowledged or worshipped in such a way.[81] He doesn't throw a petulant tantrum over Thomas' lack of belief. Jesus simply invites Thomas to investigate his wounds if he really needs to.

The proclamation that follows is not the dutiful shout of a subject worried about the angry reaction of a tyrannical leader, nor the expression of a shocked young man throwing out some ancient form of 'OMG' profanity.[82] Thomas' proclamation was the climactic response to the symphony of Jesus Christ that John has been leading his audience through, the ultimate crescendo of human revelation and confession that each of us must arrive at if we want to move from the death of our sin to the life that God has bought for us.

Many called Jesus 'Lord' before his resurrection, but none meant it to be understood as calling him God. But from Thomas' confession onwards we are left in no doubt – to declare Jesus as 'Lord' now means 'master' in its fullest sense. He is master of the destiny of humanity, as the author and saviour of life. God himself, the Lord of heaven and earth.[83]

Paul writes to the Romans, 'If you declare with your mouth, "Jesus is Lord," and believe in your heart that God raised him from the dead, you will be saved.'[84] To acknowledge Jesus in the way that Thomas did is the gateway into true life. It's the beginning of right worship of God. Theologian George Beasley-Murray comments:

> So it comes about that the most outrageous doubter of the resurrection of Jesus utters the greatest confession of the Lord who rose from the dead. His utterance does not simply acknowledge the reality of the resurrection of Jesus, but expresses its ultimate meaning…as revelation of who Jesus is. Yet it is not an abstract theological definition concerning the person of Christ. The personal pronoun is of vital importance, 'my Lord, and my God.' He confesses to the risen Jesus that he belongs to him as his willing subject; he adores him and henceforth will serve him as he deserves.[85]

FOUR: WORSHIPPER

There was no more appropriate response that could have fallen from Thomas' mouth in that moment, and it would become the defining response of his life from that moment on. Rightly worshipping Jesus changes a person.

If you've ever been awake and able to see outside when the sun rises, you will know that it is impossible to ignore what is happening. You can delight in the experience or dismiss it, but you cannot simply ignore the event. Even on the fringes of your attention you will be aware at the very least of the change in light and temperature.

Psalm 19 declares that creation itself gives revelation to the glory of God. The beauty of creation is an expression of natural worship and what we might call 'general revelation'. That is to say that anyone can see it and be moved to awe and wonder. If that awe and wonder leads them to the creator God then they have correctly understood what nature reveals.

I enjoy watching David Attenborough's natural world programmes. The camera technology seems to get better and better, as does our understanding of the natural world we observe. And yet the programmes also sadden me. So many watch these magnificently-shot images and come away with the wrong revelation. You can put the sum 'two plus two' in front of someone, but if they are unwilling or unable to follow the calculation to its obvious answer, then no matter how clear 'four' may be, they will end up with 'five'. Exploring the wonder of the world for many simply becomes a Sunday night distraction before the routine of life kicks in on Monday morning.

'Ah, what a wonderful world. Right, back to work.'

But when we truly recognise the wonder of the world as the wonder of God's creation, it becomes an opportunity for connection rather than distraction, enabling us to live in such a way that contributes to the ongoing revelation of God to a world that doesn't yet know him.

'Ah, what a wonderful God. Now, back to his work.'

Where a sunrise or any other feature of the natural world can give natural revelation of God's handiwork in creation, the church is to give supernatural revelation of Gods handiwork in our lives.[86] As the church we can be respected and treasured, despised and hated, persecuted and ridiculed, but one option that the world should never have is to ignore us. If we are truly living as the revelation of God to the world today then the church cannot be ignored.

Perhaps we as the church have made it too easy for the world to ignore us because we haven't understood what real worship is.

You don't need to be a Roman emperor to develop delusions of grandeur.[87] While the average person might not go around demanding to be called Lord and God, the Bible is clear that by missing the mark of the standard

God has set for us – to trust and worship him as Lord in every thought and action of our lives – we have essentially claimed the title for ourselves.

It's like we say, 'You might be Lord and God in 99% of my life Jesus, but I have a few notes on how to improve a couple of things on that 1%. Fix those and I'm all in.'

Our rebellion against God when we fail to trust in him perfectly is a micro-revolution against the perfect kingdom of heaven, and it leads us into worshipping something other than God. Every moment spent not trusting in God is a moment spent worshipping our own understanding, intellect, ability, desires or emotions. And it never leads to anything good. It just pulls us away from the perfect love and peace of God.

Mercifully and wonderfully, we are not abandoned by Jesus to this failure and weakness, but instead invited to meet him afresh in the forgiveness, power and grace of his resurrection. He invites us to come and investigate him again if that's what we need, to see that he is real and that he has kept his promises, and to share in his victory.

Our response to this invitation will either be trust or rebellion. We will either worship Jesus or ourselves. There is no middle ground.

We have a curious relationship with 'worship' in the church today. On the one hand you could argue that we've never been better at creatively expressing ourselves to God through song. Yet on the other, you could argue that it can become a bit one-dimensional in style and content, and worse still, that many think of worship as being a reflective time primarily for their own benefit. Failing to understand what worship really is means we will never offer God the thing that he wants far more than a song. You.

Every part of you.

People will rightly point out that the Bible encourages us to be in the habit of meeting together and to sing to the Lord. But they may not be so quick to point out that the words translated as 'worship' in the New Testament mean submission, service and reverence. If we wanted to bundle those concepts into a single word, we would perhaps be best served by 'obedience'.

Jesus is the perfect model of obedient worship, and by his death and resurrection he is the one who makes it possible for us to come back to the Father from our rebellion. Rowan Williams explains it like this:

> Jesus' sacrifice is the sacrifice of obedience. At every moment of his life he has given his heart to God in such a way that God is able to work through him with no interruption... Obedience is a harmony of response to God so that God sees in the world a reflection of his own life. Our actions in obedience reflect his... What most pleases God is God. God loves to see his selfless love reflected, to see his beauty mirrored back to him. Thus the perfect gift to God, the gift that God would really like, is God, the return to him of his own wholly generous love.[88]

FOUR: WORSHIPPER

Let us not neglect meeting together as the family of God. We've already explored some of the problems this can cause. Let us not neglect singing out joyfully (and might I suggest, thoughtfully) to our God when alone and when together as we desire to make known our love for him in any creative form that we can. But, crucially, let us not neglect giving revelation to God's glory in every part of our lives through submission, service and reverence that God would be truly glorified in our worship, and that the world would know the hope of true worship for themselves.

We are to reverently declare that Jesus is our Lord, submit to him as Lord through transformative faith that will cause the Son to rise in our lives in a way that cannot be ignored by those around us as we seek to serve him faithfully by the power of his Spirit for the eternal glory of the Father.

Thomas rightly proclaimed Jesus as Lord, but if he and his friends had not then taken that proclamation to the world through their transformed lives and teaching, then the Jesus movement would likely have been snuffed out in Jerusalem within a generation.

When we read about what happened next in the lives of those first worshippers, we see that they lived lives that couldn't be ignored. Even when it meant trouble, persecution, imprisonment, violence and death, they gave Jesus more than a verbal recognition of his lordship, more than a song. They gave him themselves.

In a sermon given in 1955, Billy Graham powerfully expressed the reality of whole-life worship:

> A true sacrament is not a mere creed, or ordinance, or form, but it is a life of service to God and to man. The most eloquent prayer is the prayer through hands that heal and bless. The highest form of worship is the worship of unselfish Christian service. The greatest form of praise is the sound of consecrated feet seeking out the lost and helpless.[89]

In Billy Graham we saw a life that lived out those words.

My friend Chrissy felt the call of God on her life when she was a young woman to take the gospel to the Philippines. Chrissy was just an ordinary girl from Manchester who loved Jesus, and out of her worship of him couldn't stand the thought of Filipino people suffering in poverty, children without a family to look after them, or prisoners without hope in prison.

In the early days Chrissy couldn't get access to the prisons so she would go and stand outside the prison walls and sing worship songs and preach the gospel until she saw hands poke through the bars in response. Over time opportunities came for her to go inside and minister directly – something that she still does today, more than thirty-five years later. Chrissy set up homes for the children of inmates (who were either abandoned or forced to live in prison with their parents) and children with disabilities, and runs a school that offers free private education to hundreds of children who would otherwise go without.[90]

I remember visiting a small village with Chrissy that had been destroyed by a landslide a couple of years earlier. Chrissy and her team had relocated entire families into new housing and were taking care of various practical needs, but also leading Bible classes and preaching the gospel regularly. Singing songs of worship to God with inmates in the prisons, with the children in the homes and in that village will live long in my memory. These were people connected to their creator in worship because of one person who had chosen to give her life in obedient worship to her king.

Whether you're called to serve in another nation like Chrissy, or to become a great itinerant preaching evangelist like Billy Graham, or to serve as a teacher or a stay-at-home parent, or to work in business or in any other vocation, you are first called to be a worshipper because you were first created to be a worshipper. A. W. Tozer asks:

On Monday, as we go about our different duties and tasks, are we aware of the presence of God? The Lord desires still to be in his holy temple, wherever we are. He wants the continuing love and delight and worship of his children, wherever we work. Is it not a beautiful thing for a businessman to enter his office on Monday morning with an inner call to worship... If you cannot worship the Lord in the midst of your responsibilities on Monday, it is not very likely that you were worshipping on Sunday![91]

The crescendo of the symphony continues on from our proclamation of Jesus as 'my Lord and my God' into the life that follows, mirroring the life of our saviour himself.

The world can ignore the church getting together merely to sing our own songs and create our own subculture, but it cannot ignore us as the transformed people of God declaring 'my Lord and my God' with every action of our lives.

It's almost impossible to ignore the people of God who worshipfully return God's love to him by clothing the poor, feeding the hungry and taking care of the sick, who return God's love to him by counting the cost of truly loving others, and who return God's love to him by reaching out to the least, the last and the lost with the hope and saving power of the gospel.

Our lives offered back to God in sacrificial obedience is the worshipful crescendo of gospel revelation to a world singing the wrong song.

FOUR: WORSHIPPER

CHAPTER FOUR: DISCUSSION QUESTIONS

What does it mean for Jesus to truly be Lord?

How would you define true worship of God?

What would the un-ignorable church look like?

How might our worship gatherings (church or otherwise) fuel us for our worshipful service in the world?

CHAPTER FOUR: APPLICATION

As you live out your faith daily and offer Jesus to those around you, keep a journal or notes on your phone of the encounters, conversations and fruit that you experience. Once a week look back at these and use them as points of thanksgiving and praise to God who provided the opportunity and who is faithfully at work in it even when your engagement with the person has ended, which will also be a reminder to keep praying for those you encounter.

FIVE
QUESTIONER

*Thomas said to him, 'Lord, we don't know where
you are going, so how can we know the way?'*
JOHN 14:5

Silence. Nothing but awkward silence filled the air in the
moments after I finished my garbled response to the tutor's
question. A group of colleagues and I were receiving some
specialist evangelism training and the guest tutor had asked
if any of us knew what a particular missional model was.
Wanting to be the smart one in the room I nodded my head
as if to say, 'I don't know about the rest of these part-timers,
but you and I are on the same page, buddy.' Truth be told,
I had at least heard of the model, but I couldn't have told
you how it worked. I certainly hadn't expected him to ask
me to explain my understanding to the rest of the class.
Three minutes of me trying to save face later, and everyone
sat there silently, reflecting no doubt on how they would

ever move past the awkwardness so that they could make conversation with me again in the staff kitchen.

Few of us enjoy being put on the spot by a tricky question, especially when we don't have an answer to offer. But I'm not sure that we always have the healthiest relationship with questions at the best of times. Some consider the idea of asking challenging questions in their church community as a one-way ticket to being declared a heretic, and so never do. Others make a sport of it, where being seen to be the cleverest in the room becomes more important than a sincere journey towards God's truth.

Then there's the challenge of putting our faith on display to the world only to be confronted with a barrage of questions in return, many of which we don't always feel equipped to answer. Some Christians become convinced that they will do more harm than good in being available to answer the questions of those around them and so for that reason keep a relatively low faith profile. But the world does have questions. We have questions![92]

The disciples had questions too of course, and it can be easy to read the gospels and feel a little envious of their access to the rabbi of all rabbis. Whenever a difficult question arose they could ask Jesus face-to-face for an answer and hear directly from their teacher. Then again, Jesus didn't always give a straightforward answer, and he often preferred to ask another question in response.

In John 14 we find Jesus with his disciples on the night of his arrest, sharing with them some of his most profound and difficult teaching. Their heads are spinning (poor old Peter is particularly vexed, having been told by Jesus that he's cashing boldness cheques that will bounce not once but three times). Then Jesus starts talking about going away. There is talk of his Father's house, of preparing a place for the disciples, and of the fact that they know the way to where he is going. Thomas is quick to articulate the confusion they all shared by asking Jesus a question: 'Erm, Jesus, we don't actually know where it is that you are going, so how can we possibly know the way?'

Have you ever played charades and hit the point of utter frustration when, even though you are currently out-acting Meryl Streep, the guesses of your dim-witted friends are nowhere near what you are trying to convey? I wonder if that's how Jesus felt a lot of the time when he was teaching his disciples, who so routinely seemed to miss the point (to be fair, I'm sure we wouldn't have done any better).

And yet, Jesus doesn't call Thomas an idiot and storm out of the room in frustration like we might during family games night. He also doesn't use his regular trick of answering a question with another question. This is one of the rare occasions on which Jesus gives his friends a straight answer to the question asked: 'I am the way, the truth and the life. No one comes to the Father except through me.'

Or to put it another way: 'I am the answer to your question, Thomas.'

In the previous chapter we looked at the opening words of Psalm 19. If we had continued, we would have discovered that God has blessed us with more than just general revelation to point us in the right direction, we also have the special revelation of his holy word to tell us exactly who he is.

'Who can discern their own errors?' the psalmist asks. That's a good question. By what standard do we work out if we are on the right track, or going the right way? God has provided us with his word through which we can know more than what right is, we can know who he is. The psalmist writes,

> The law of the Lord is perfect,
>   refreshing the soul.
> The statutes of the Lord are trustworthy,
>   making wise the simple.
> The precepts of the Lord are right,
>   giving joy to the heart.
> The commands of the Lord are radiant,
>   giving light to the eyes.[93]

The word 'law' used here is translated from the word *Torah*. *Torah* basically means 'instruction', and while it is often used to describe the first five books of the Old Testament (the Pentateuch) it can have a wider meaning that encompasses all of God's instruction, teaching and law. *Torah* is the perfect instruction of God about himself, given to his people, the Israelites, the story of which continues into the

New Testament as the fulfilment of the promises that God had made. This is God's story.

And yet every person has in some way decided to promote themselves to become the hero of their own life, and our rejection of God as the author and hero of the story has led us to ruin. We've scribbled discordance, incoherence and obscenity across the pages of God's perfect manuscript of life in an attempt to rewrite it to our own taste and preference. We've ruined it.

To top it all off, being the hero of our own story doesn't turn out how we hoped it would. We try to make sense of the senseless scrawling that we've produced, but we create more confusion. We ask questions of identity, of purpose, of fulfilment, of love and of hope:

'Which way?'

'Which truth?'

'Which life?'

And just when it looks like these questions will go unanswered, the author himself steps into the story:

'I am the way, the truth and the life.'

FIVE: QUESTIONER

Jesus is the living *Torah*. Not someone who merely knows the way. He is the way. He says, 'I am the answer to your question, world.'

This special revelation of Jesus and the provision of his truth in the Bible has made it possible for us to not only know who God is, but to actually know him and to be in relationship with him. We can make sense of who we are as his creation, and discover the framework he has called us to live within and why. We can hear the call to repent for what it is, stop running away, and through Jesus know the way back to the Father, the perfect author of life.

As we are 'instructed' by Jesus, the living *Torah*, in the pages of his holy word, we find the hope of refreshment for our souls, the blessing of heavenly wisdom, the possibility of joy in every circumstance, and the provision of new perspective as the light of God shines into the darkness.

As we explore God's special revelation we begin to find answers to our questions. Actually, we are doing theology.

People can get a bit twitchy about the idea of theology. I suspect it's mainly because they misunderstand what theology is. St Anselm famously said that theology is simply 'faith seeking understanding.' Any time we make a statement or ask a question about our faith we are doing theology. Or as my dad likes to say: 'Every Christian is a theologian. The only question is are you going to be a good one or a bad one?'

Theology isn't about being the smartest person in the room. Jesus certainly didn't seem interested in that kind of thing. Jesus was interested in revealing himself to be the truth. As I seek understanding in my faith, as I explore his word, I don't want the discoveries of my journey to point to me being the smartest person in the room, I want my discoveries to help me more fully know Jesus as being the way, the truth and the life and to reveal him as such to the world. I want my theology – my 'faith seeking understanding' – to truly discover Jesus as the answer.

Asking good questions about God, our lives and the reality of our human experience is exactly what we should be doing as we seek to know God more, and to live well in his story. But if we want to do it well, to honour God as we go, if we want to be good theologians rather than bad ones, then we would be wise to approach the word of God in four simple ways.

PROVISION: THE REFRESHMENT OF DAILY BREAD

If you've ever gone without food for a little while you may have experienced hunger pangs. I remember a series of television adverts for a particular breakfast cereal brand that visualised this idea by showing people going about their daily activities only to have a cartoon hunger monster jump out and tap on their stomach with a couple of spoons while shouting, 'Hunger strikes!' It sounds weirder than it actually was. Of course the solution to getting the weird cartoon hunger monster off your case and to avoid those hunger pangs was to eat the cereal.

I wonder if you've ever experienced Bible pangs? Jesus says that we aren't to live by bread alone which nourishes us physically, but by the word of God which nourishes us spiritually.[94] Do you realise your need for his word? Do you satisfy that need by taking a quick snack here and there, or by taking the time to prepare and indulge in a feast?

Writing in her helpful book *Reading The Bible With Rabbi Jesus*, Lois Tverberg makes this sharp observation:

> A lot of us do Bible study microwave-style. We gulp down a prepackaged, presweetened devotion with a few slurps of coffee before heading off to work. Is it at all surprising when it's bland and unmemorable, like a vending-machine sandwich?[95]

There's nothing wrong with a good Bible devotional. They can be extremely helpful as part of our ongoing engagement with God's word. But the word of God is spiritual food that is best feasted upon slowly rather than gobbled as a quick snack. This feasting involves not only reading, but praying too. It involves asking God to read with us, to illuminate his truth as we go. Praying the words of scripture when our own words fail. Giving thanks for the joy and hope of what we discover. Seeking forgiveness as the word illuminates our darkness. Asking God to help us to turn the words we read into worshipful living.

The more we journey with Jesus, the more we come to realise our need for him, and that includes our need and desire to know him through his word. Your questions can be asked in its pages and, while there will be challenges along the way and confusion here and there – or even perhaps silence at times – the author of life has promised to read it with you as you discover the full reality of Jesus as the ultimate answer day by day.

Pray. Read. Feast daily and be refreshed.

PERSPECTIVE: ILLUMINATED BY GOD'S PROMISES

When the two disciples on the road to Emmaus met the resurrected Jesus, not recognising him, they were amazed that this stranger seemed unaware of the events that had just taken place in Jerusalem.[96]

As the journey continues, the disciples explain the Easter events, including the fact that on that very morning their friends had visited Jesus' tomb to find it empty and encountered angels instead! Suddenly the disciples' amazement at the stranger's lack of awareness was replaced by Jesus' own. He rebukes them for misunderstanding the word of God. He doesn't rebuke to embarrass or shame them, but to reveal his disapproval of their lack of trust in God's promises. New Testament scholar James Edwards explains:

Jesus does not rebuke the disciples for disbelieving the evidence associated with the resurrection, or for disbelieving the witness of the women, or even for not recognizing himself. He rebukes them for reading the Scriptures without understanding and belief. The disciples' problem is not one of head, but of heart. Mary was blessed because she believed the Lord would fulfil his promises to her.[97]

As the old saying goes, 'Be careful not to have the whole Bible in your head, yet not one verse in your heart.'

How we understand the 'big picture' story of God will affect how we understand the word of God as a whole and how we apply it to our lives.[98] We often focus more on the essential truths than the big story, and we become prone to proof-texting – taking a verse out of context to make it say what we want it to say, or what we feel that it says. While we need to know the essential truths of the Bible so that we can live in God's truth, those truths only make sense within the big story of God, past, present and future. The Bible can be hard to understand sometimes, so trying to understand its truth while, for example, only reading the 'easier' New Testament is like trying to shred a Jimi Hendrix guitar solo with your hands tied behind your back. The gospel itself has been frequently misunderstood for precisely this reason.

Untie your hands. Commit to treating the word of God as a whole and bring into focus the full story of God, through which you will make sense of his promises and understand his essential truth more fully.

The word of God gives us all his fixed promises to which we can hold on in every season and circumstance. It also confronts us, like those disciples on the road to Emmaus, with necessary rebuke as we realise we have failed to trust in God, and have fallen into trusting the answer of an idol somewhere in our lives. This rebuke is not designed by God to put us to shame, but by his disapproval he points us to a better answer. The light of his sight can be restored to our presently sin-darkened eyes.

When confronted with the rebuke of Jesus, we must repent. We've been going the wrong way. We must let his word give us the foundation upon which to understand his big story, to course-correct our lives, to reset our perspectives, to fix our illuminated eyes on the blessed assurance of his faithfulness, even in our failure.[99]

PROTECTION: WISELY WIELDING THE WEAPON

When the devil confronts Jesus at the climax of his forty days in the wilderness, he employs all of his best temptation techniques to draw Jesus away from worshipful obedience to the Father (that is always his aim). Jesus' response is to wield the weapon of scripture to defend against the schemes of the enemy, and, sure enough, Satan retreats.[100] Jesus feasted on the provision of the word and allowed it to set his perspective, which meant he was ready when Satan came calling.

The word of God is our defence against the attacks of the enemy. Upon its truth we build our faith which helps us extinguish the fiery arrows that come our way. But importantly it is also the gateway to wisdom, which we need to discern how to wield the weapon of the word correctly. This is not a weapon to be used against people (as it has often been abused), but against the powers and principalities of darkness that pull people away from their loving creator God.[101]

When Satan seeks to usurp Jesus by throwing a question of temptation, doubt or accusation your way, be sure to answer him with the mighty power of God's unchanging word.

PROCLAMATION: LIVING AND SHARING TRUE JOY

We don't have a perfect understanding of every part of the truth. John reminds us in his gospel that when Jesus rode into Jerusalem on a donkey, while a great crowd gave Jesus a king's welcome with shouts of 'Hosanna!' the disciples themselves were left a bit perplexed by the whole thing. It was only after his resurrection that they were able to make sense of what had happened.[102]

Many elements of God's truth take time to understand. Others require us to accept that God is beyond our complete understanding. But that should never deter us from going into the world to point to Jesus as the way, the truth and the life. We should also remember that the word of God itself is living and active, and able by the power of the Holy Spirit to provide its own answers far more effectively than we can at times.

My friend Lauren came to see me one day in a state of concern and frustration. Her grandmother was sick and there were fears that she might not live for long. Lauren was concerned because her grandmother had never been interested in faith, and frustrated because, despite various efforts over the years, and even though she was a gifted evangelist, Lauren hadn't yet seen her grandmother give her life to Jesus.

Lauren asked me a question: 'My gran is dying, what can I do to help her know Jesus before she does?'

Having asked Lauren to explain to me the journey and what she had done so far, I only had two suggestions for her.

'First, you should pray for and with your gran,' I said. 'Prayer is the bedrock of evangelism, after all the power of salvation belongs to God, not us, so let's put the power where the power belongs.'

Lauren nodded and said that she prayed for her gran every day and at regular opportunities had asked her gran if they could pray together, with mixed results.

'Okay,' I said, 'Keep doing that. But have you ever just asked your gran if she wants to read the Bible with you?'

Lauren looked at me as if she wasn't entirely sure that I was being serious. I was.

'Seriously, tell her about how you read the Bible every day, and reading it with her would be one way you could spend more time together. Plus, there might be some things she can help you understand in there with a fresh perspective. Invite her into the journey.'

And so, sure enough, that's what Lauren did. Just over a week later I got a message from Lauren saying that her gran had moved closer to Jesus in the last ten days of Bible study than she had in the last ten years of her other evangelistic efforts. Lauren's gran was even texting her throughout the day asking what this or that meant – she was reading the Bible even when Lauren wasn't around. The word of God is living and active.[103]

Don't be afraid of reading the Bible with people who may then raise questions to which you don't know the answer. We can easily get hung up on *what* we don't know and forget that it's actually about *who* we do know. Reading the word of God is not supposed to give you knowledge of something, it gives you knowledge of someone.

The psalmist goes on to declare in Psalm 19 that the word of God is more precious than gold and sweeter than honey. The word of God is the most precious gift to us because by it we can know him. I wonder whether you consider the Bible to be precious in this way.

Precious as it was to Bible translators John Wycliffe and William Tyndale, who were prepared to risk the charge of heresy and the punishment of death to produce the first English Bibles that could be read by the common person. Tyndale's commitment to get the scriptures into the hands of ordinary people was best summed up in his famous response to one opponent who held that the decrees of the church (specifically the Pope) were a high enough connection to God's word for the common man: 'If God spare my life, ere many years I will cause a boy who drives a plough to know more of the scriptures than you.'[104] Tyndale certainly got the scriptures into such hands, but at the cost of his reputation, his freedom and ultimately his life.

Precious as it was to Open Doors founder Brother Andrew, who risked his life time and again to smuggle Bibles behind the Iron Curtain and into China and Cuba so that believers in those communist nations could have access to the word of God for themselves. Or Voice of the Martyrs founder Richard Wurmbrand who was imprisoned and horrifically tortured for years by the oppressive regime of the Soviet Union for his preaching and distribution of the word of God.[105] Wurmbrand's unwavering commitment to the word traced back to his own conversion years earlier when he had received and read a Bible 'written not so much in words, but in flames of love' from an elderly Christian couple who then led him to Christ.[106]

Precious as it was to persecuted Chinese pastor Brother Yun who was so desperate for a Bible when he became a Christian as a teenager that he prayed and fasted for one hundred days (only eating a simple bowl of rice each night), asking that the Lord might provide him with one. He wrote, 'I was so hungry for a Bible… I prayed for a Bible until I could bear it no more… Looking back years later I would say this whole experience was the most difficult thing I've ever endured.'[107] A man who was imprisoned and tortured for his faith found the most challenging experience of his life not to be those awful events, or his unfulfilled hunger for food in the long days of fasting, but his unfulfilled hunger for the word of God.

The majority of us have access to the Bible in our pockets via our phones wherever and whenever we want and never face the kind of threats to our freedom, our health or our lives that these people faced. Instead of getting comfortable with what we have and neglecting it, we should treat every encounter with the word of God as an invitation to feast with Jesus.

Brother Yun was eventually blessed with a Bible and his response was almost as precious as the gift he received:

> I clutched my new Bible to my heart and fell down on my knees… I thanked God again and again! I promised Jesus that from that moment on I would devour his word like a hungry child.[108]

We needn't be envious of the disciples' access to Jesus because he makes himself available to us all through his word and by his Spirit. He invites us to ask him our questions, to devour his word like hungry children and to discover him afresh.

The living *Torah* invites us to speak to him daily in prayer and know him daily in his word in order that we might live in him. That we would become the living *Torah* ourselves, witnesses to the world that Jesus is the answer. It has been said that you might be the only Bible someone ever reads. Through fellowship with the living *Torah* we grow into ever more beautiful translations of his truth.

In Shūsaku Endō's remarkable novel *Silence*, the Jesuit priest Sebastião Rodrigues, on a dangerous and prohibited Christian mission to Japan in the seventeenth century, is confronted with the harsh persecution of Japanese believers, tortured into renouncing their faith by the authorities. Throughout the novel the question of God's seeming silence in the face of the suffering of his people is raised, and as the story draws to a close, Rodrigues is still haunted by this question.

And then, all of a sudden, Jesus speaks, giving Rodrigues his answer. It turns out to be the same answer he gave to Thomas centuries earlier: 'I was not silent, I suffered beside you.' Or to put it another way, 'I am the answer to your question, Sebastião.'

Jesus' reply to the question raised by the suffering of the world changes everything. He did not stay silent, but stepped into the mess of our sin and its chaotic consequences in order to suffer with us, until the day that he suffered for us. His shout of *tetelestai* upon the cross is the final word to the question that all humanity is asking. Is there hope of rescue from our sin and suffering?

Jesus says, 'It is finished.' He is the answer, and he answers you personally.

The final words of Endo's novel are breathtaking. Rodrigues moves from hearing Jesus' answer to living in it:

> [Rodrigues] loved him now in a different way from before. Everything that had taken place until now had been necessary to bring him to this love… 'Our Lord was not silent. Even if he had been silent, my life until this day would have spoken of him.'[109]

Jesus isn't threatened by our questions. He doesn't mind being put on the spot. He is never left without an answer to give. Sometimes his answer is found in the seeming silence. Ravi Zacharias explains that sometimes we have to 'learn the hard way that God's answers are not always propositional. Sometimes they are only heard in our relationship to him and in his presence within us. He conquers not in spite of our pain but through it."[110]

Through it all Jesus continually points us to the singular reality that he is the way, the truth and the life in the living and active pages of scripture and through the tangible impact of his lordship in our lives. As we hear his answer for what it truly is, we can learn to love God in a new way, to trust him more completely and grow as a people whose lives speak of him as the answer. People of the way. People of the truth. People of the life.

The world has many questions. May we know our Lord more and more through his word as we address our own questions, and would his transforming truth and presence in our lives be seen by the world for what it is – the answer by which they too may become people of the way, the truth and the life, today and forevermore.

FIVE: QUESTIONER

CHAPTER FIVE: DISCUSSION QUESTIONS

What is the one question you would ask God if you knew he would answer you right now?

Are you noticing certain questions come up regularly amongst your not-yet-Christian friends?

What is your daily Bible engagement like? Do you need to make more time to feast?

What does it truly mean for Jesus to be the way, the truth, and the life as you trust in him and tell the world of his love?

CHAPTER FIVE: APPLICATION

Ask a not-yet-Christian friend if they would ever be interested in reading the Bible with you. Start with one of the gospels and make it a genuine learning experience for both of you. Invite questions, offer your own, and ask the Lord to speak to you and your friend through his precious word as you go.

SIX
ADVENTURER

Then Thomas (also known as Didymus) said to the rest of
the disciples, 'Let us also go, that we may die with him.'
JOHN 11:16

Who doesn't enjoy jumping into a dangerous adventure
in the pages of an exciting novel or at the cinema? When
it comes to real life, though, I'm less inclined to head off
into the wilderness in search of the kind of death-defying
activity that Bear Grylls might eat for breakfast (if he's not
already eating bugs or some other weird wilderness snack).

Some people's lives seem to be driven by adventure.
I recently watched the documentary *Free Solo* in which
climber Alex Honnold attempted to climb the 900-metre
vertical rockface of El Capitan in Yosemite national park
without rope or harness.[111] The tiniest mistake over the
three-hour-plus climb would have meant certain death for

SIX: ADVENTURER

Honnold who was at times hanging onto the rockface quite literally by his fingertips.

Then there are those adventurers who, when adventure turns to crisis, are able to do something above and beyond, like cutting off their own trapped arm in order to escape a slow and certain death.[112] Those are the kind of people whose life stories make for inspirational movies that get us all thinking: what would I do in that situation? I'd probably be dead in the movie version before anyone had cleared the first few handfuls of popcorn.

Even the most adventure-happy among us might look at the activities of some of these adventurers and think they are crazy to go quite that far. And some look at the actions of the apostles throughout the book of Acts in the same way – suggesting that they were simply the crazy 'out there' ones on the extreme end of the spectrum of gospel adventure.

We could look at a free solo climber like Alex Honnold and, while impressed by his skill and courage, walk away thinking, 'No thanks, not for me.' And we're under no compulsion or obligation to risk our lives in that way. But when it comes to the activity of the apostles, it becomes problematic when we look at their lives and think, 'Count me out.'

In John 11, Jesus finds out that his dear friend Lazarus is extremely sick. Jesus doesn't panic. He declares that the sickness will not end in death. The disciples must have been relieved to hear this – not least because they wouldn't have wanted Lazarus to die, but also because, if the sickness had been serious enough, then Jesus might have been tempted to go and see Lazarus in Judea, a place where very recently he had almost been stoned to death by his opponents during the Festival of Dedication.

There was probably an audible sigh of relief as the disciples realised that Jesus wasn't thinking of taking them back into the lion's den to visit Lazarus. Jesus had poked that particular lion on their last visit and the lion was probably still agitated. Better to steer clear. But a couple of days later, that sigh of relief would turn into a cry of protest.

No sooner had the disciples begun to make their not-re-turning-to-Judea-to-get-stoned-to-death party plans than Jesus was telling them that they were in fact going to Judea to see Lazarus after all. Predictably enough, the disciples were baffled and concerned by his decision to walk back into the danger zone. The disciples appear to be so wrapped up in nervousness about returning to Judea that they missed what Jesus was telling them about the seriousness of Lazarus' condition. Their question seems justified: 'Jesus, why do we need to risk our lives to be Lazarus' alarm clock?'

It's not unreasonable that the disciples misunder-stood Jesus' use of the sleep metaphor to explain Lazarus' condition, but, cryptic or not, it's always harder to discern the truth when your mind is elsewhere, foggy with fear or concern. This is especially true when Jesus is not expressing something plainly, but profoundly as he leads us into a fuller truth.

Jesus clarifies. Lazarus is dead. At this point, Thomas pipes up in a way that I'm sure made some of the other disciples give him the 'stop talking' eyes that spouses develop in a marriage for use during dinner parties: 'Come on lads, let's go and die with Jesus!'

Some scholars are quick to label Thomas' words as the expression of a pessimist, which seems unnecessarily harsh. Generally pessimists use negative forecasting to avoid or dissuade others from engaging in something. But I see no reason to read anything other than sincerity in Thomas' words. He's ready to follow Jesus wherever it takes him, even to death. Thomas has, unwittingly at least, just proclaimed in the most profound way the full reality of what following Jesus means.

Thomas encourages the other disciples to go 'all in' with Jesus, even if it costs them their lives. Little did he know that it would be Jesus who would first go 'all in' for us by giving his life so that we could know true life. Thomas certainly hadn't made that deeper connection while in his moment of despair after the crucifixion – when he could only see death as an end, as failure. But Jesus would recon-figure all of that by showing in his resurrection that his death was in fact his victory.

And it is in this victorious death that Jesus invites each of us to trust and share, that we might live. Bonhoeffer famously expressed it in writing: 'When Christ calls a man, he bids him come and die.'[113] If you want true life, Jesus tells his followers, then you must lose yours.[114] The ultimate adventure according to Jesus is to follow him into the grave and come out the other side as a new creation. It's an adventure that we mark in the profound symbolism of baptism.

When Jesus arrived at Lazarus' grave he said to Martha, 'I am the resurrection and the life. The one who believes in me will live, even though they die; and whoever lives by believing in me will never die. Do you believe this?'[115]

Jesus then called Lazarus out of the grave and into life.

Every time the disciples reveal themselves to be a bit dense, proud, or cowardly in the gospel stories, it serves to make their eventual transformation into bold, world-changing gospel ninjas all the more amazing.[116] When Peter and John are hauled before the Sanhedrin, it's easy to forget that just a few weeks earlier Peter had three times fearfully denied knowing Jesus while on the outskirts of the Sanhedrin court and, arguably, while he was in little actual danger from admitting his association with Jesus. Now he and John are centre stage in court proceedings and refusing to bow to any decree that would stop them from proclaiming the gospel in word and deed, no matter the punishment or cost.

The Sanhedrin officials were astonished. They had no idea what to make of these ordinary and unschooled men who stood before them with such courage and boldness, except to note that 'they had been with Jesus.'[117]

Once you've been with Jesus, nothing is ever the same. As the gospel truly gets under your skin it inspires and empowers even the most risk-averse person to go and evangelistically free solo the El Capitan opportunity before them.

Speaking of rockfaces, a couple of years ago I took a short holiday with a couple of friends who are definitely in the adventurer category. They convinced me that climbing up a volcano would be fun, and even though my idea of adventure is mainly based around trying out new coffee shops, I decided to give it a go.

The climb up was fine, dare I say it, fun even. But after taking in the view at the top, one friend suggested a 'short cut' to get back down. Can I offer you a little advice at this point? Don't take a shortcut from the top of a volcano, especially one suggested by someone making up the route as they go.

Thirty minutes later, I found myself clinging to the side of a sheer rock face wondering why *National Geographic* weren't there to document my own (in)glorious free solo attempt. To be fair, there was a lot less crying involved when Alex Honnold did it.

I was stuck, unsure about where to place my feet next and very aware that a wrong move might lead to my falling a long way down. A really long way. In the meantime, my shortcut-suggesting friend (who by this point I had discovered was half man, half mountain goat) was moving freely around the rocks without a care in the world, as if impervious to the possibility of slipping and getting hurt, which only made me feel worse. I made it down eventually but it was a deeply uncomfortable experience throughout.

There are many Christians who, when faced with the idea of evangelism, are like me on the way down that volcano. They are paralysed by the fear of putting a foot wrong and falling in some way – losing friends, socially embarrassing themselves, or even letting God down – all while comparing themselves unfavourably to those running around them who seem to be complete naturals.

Then there are others who didn't even make it to the rockface in the first place, too comfortable in their current routine to take on the adventure, and dare I say it, somewhat indifferent about those who don't know Jesus.

The great missionary William Carey lamented that, 'Multitudes sit at ease and give themselves no concern about the far greater part of their fellow sinners, who to this day, are lost in ignorance and idolatry.'[118] I fear that this two hundred-year-old lament is still far too relevant today. But it doesn't have to be this way.

Gladys Aylward (1902–1970) had been kicked out of her missionary Bible school for failing to hit the necessary grades, and had been told on numerous occasions to give up her dream of being a missionary in China. While Christianity had at one time bored Gladys, who wanted more than anything at that time to be an actress, one night, and for reasons she couldn't explain, Gladys ended up at a Christian meeting where she was so profoundly affected by the gospel that she gave her life to Jesus. Her heart for the lost and a desire to become a missionary to China came soon after her radical turn to Christ.

Now, here she was, a twenty-seven-year-old woman without a missionary organisation behind her, uneducated and unfunded, but unwilling to ignore the call to gospel adventure. She laid her Bible and the small amount of money she had to her name on her bed and prayed a simple prayer: 'Here is my Bible. Here is all the money I have. Here is me. Please use me, God!'[119]

Through a remarkable story of complete commitment to following God's call and his provision for her along the way, in 1932 Gladys eventually made it to China (although the story of getting there was a lifetime's adventure in itself). As the only Westerner within a two-day donkey ride of the remote town she came to call home, Yangcheng, Gladys served God as faithfully as she could while faced with an alien culture, a language barrier, financial strain, and the threat of violence and even death.

One day, many months later, Gladys was visited by the Mandarin, the local government official for the district who was a very powerful man with the authority to exercise the death penalty as he saw fit. Fearing that she may be in some sort of trouble with this official, Gladys braced herself for the encounter, only to be presented with an opportunity she could never have foreseen or planned for.

The practice of foot binding (a barbaric custom to make girls' feet smaller and more 'desirable') had been banned by the Chinese government and this now needed enforcing. It was culturally inappropriate for a man to do this job, and all the women in the towns were unable to traverse the vast ground that needed covering because of their own damaged feet. Gladys was the only suitable candidate.

Gladys accepted, but on one condition – that she could share her faith openly wherever she went:

> ...for months and then years I travelled around to village after village until I became known and welcomed and made many friends. I was called 'The Storyteller' and the villagers never tired of hearing the Old Testament stories told over and over again. As I look back, I am amazed at the way God opened up the opportunities for service. I had longed to go to China, but never in my wildest dreams had I imagined that God would overrule in such a way that I would be given entrance into every village home; have authority to banish a cruel, horrible custom; have government protection; and be paid to preach the gospel of Jesus Christ as I inspected feet! Gradually there were ones and twos converted here and there and in each village a little group gathered – the beginning of a small church. So through the next years as the gospel was preached, the practice of foot-binding ceased, opium-taking was reduced,

and a witness to the saving grace of Jesus Christ was set up in many places.[120]

And it all started with a simple prayer of availability. 'Here is my Bible. Here is all the money I have. Here is me. Please use me, God!'

There are those whose lives obviously look like adventure, such as Gladys Aylward and the apostles before her. But adventure is subjective. Comfortable and ordinary for one person can be uncomfortable and extraordinary for another.

When I first met Amanda, she had not long before become a follower of Jesus while attending an Alpha course at her local church. Within weeks of the course, Amanda was reaching out to her neighbours with the good news of Jesus through simple acts of kindness and practical support, offering to pray, and whatever explanation of the gospel she could manage in those encounters. Amanda had embraced the primary adventure of death to self and everyday trust in Jesus, and the adventure of sharing the gospel that follows for all believers. Amanda's prayer of availability might have gone something like this: 'Here is my street. Here is me. Please use me, God!'

Whether called to foreign lands or the street on which you have lived your whole life, God is asking if you are available to him. If you are afraid, will you trust in his power and provision as you take your next step? If you are blunted by comparison, will you allow God to tell a unique story in and through your life? If you are trapped in comfort and apathy, will you let God break your heart for the lost? Are you available to become who you were created to be, his image-bearer in this world?

The Bible's idea of what it means to be created in the image of God is far more sophisticated and profound than our well-intentioned 'you are fearfully and wonderfully made' encouragements often reveal. One of the challenges faced by the Jews was suspicion from other religions about their lack of an idol to worship. Pagan temples were filled with all sorts of idols and images of the gods to be worshipped, but the Jews were forbidden from creating an image of the living God and their synagogues and temple contained no such image. Tom Wright comments:

> Our God, the Jews would have said, is the One God who made the whole world. He cannot be represented by a human-made image. We will demonstrate who he is by the way we live.[121]

The effect of the risen Jesus on a person's life is that we move from misunderstanding God and ourselves to being known by the creator and king, to being given new life and new identity. It's not as simple as a fresh start, it is God taking who you already are and doing something new with it.

In our disposable world, when something seems broken we tend to throw it away and get something new. That doesn't just apply to the things we own, but our relationships too. Scrapping it all and starting again is often seen as the easier or better way. But God does something harder and more glorious. He takes all your mess, failure and weakness and says, 'Watch me do something new with this in my power, grace and love.'

He's not going to scrap our world and start again. He promised Noah that he wouldn't do that after the great flood. Likewise, he's not going to scrap your life and start again.[122] He's going to redeem it. He's going to transform what you once were into what you should always have been as you choose to die to the old way of existing in your own power and step into the newness of life in his power.

We can move from isolation to relationship with the eternal triune God, adopted into his everlasting family, outworked on earth today in the form of the church. We can be daily healed of our brokenness, forgiven of our sin, moved beyond our rebellion, our failure, our hurt and our fear and into new life as new creations by God's wonderful grace.

God invites us to know him, which means being inquisitive about him, asking questions about his truth so that we might grow in our knowledge of him. He invites us to worship him for who is really is – the one true God of all creation, the perfect loving Father who has rescued us from death.

The greatest adventure we could ever pursue is to follow Jesus into the fullness of our declaration of 'my Lord and my God' and the life that follows. That we would die so that he might live in us.

In Mark's gospel we read that wonderful story of the friends who brought their paralysed friend to Jesus for healing.[123] The problem is that they can't get into the house because it's so full of people who want an audience with Jesus. Undeterred, they head up to the roof and engage in what I can only describe as an act of holy vandalism as they rip off the roofing to create a hole through which to lower their friend into the room. Don't you just love their desperation to get their buddy in front of Jesus! As Jesus forgives and heals their friend, transforming his life in the now and in the eternal, we see that their hope was not misplaced.

Are you desperate to get people in front of Jesus? Desperate because we know what he has done for us, and we know that any person who can be brought into the presence of the risen Jesus can know his forgiveness, his healing touch, his redeeming power? It might take years, it might cost us everything in the task, but he is mighty to save.

Gladys Aylward's relationship with the Mandarin developed over time into a genuine friendship. The Mandarin would tell Gladys of his admiration for her, but also share his belief that her Christian mission was futile and would have less of an effect than 'a gnat landing on the surface of the ocean.'

SIX: ADVENTURER

Whether through our own frailty, the pressures of the world, or the schemes of the enemy, sometimes that's what we can end up thinking too.

'It's futile.'

'It's too dangerous.'

'It's too costly.'

'God hasn't called me with all my weakness and fear.'

'God doesn't use people like me with all my sin and failure.'

'God couldn't use someone like me with my limited ability and lack of gifting.'

Some years later and in the middle of a war that threatened all that Gladys had built to reach out to the Chinese, the Mandarin came to see her one last time:

'I have watched you ever since you came… You love all our people, and you work hard for them.'
'It is God's will that I do so, Mandarin.'
'That I have come to know. Before I leave, I would like to be received into your church and worship the God you worship. Will you grant this?'

'God will grant it, Mandarin,' I replied, my eyes full of tears. In the midst of all this suffering and privation, my God was still working. After years of sowing the seed, He was allowing me to see it bear fruit in the heart of this honoured and powerful representative of Old China.[124]

The uneducated, unfunded, missionary society reject.

Sometimes we never see the fruit of our labour. At other times we do, but it takes years of waiting. In every outcome, God is faithful, and he is delighted to use uneducated, unfunded, seemingly unimportant and unlikely people to reveal his great faithfulness to the world. None of those things are a barrier to God, but our unavailability is. God simply wants to know if you are available for the adventure. If you are, he can take care of everything else.

Free solo climbers take on their adventures without rope or harness. But we head into the greatest adventure this side of eternity in the loving harness of heavenly power. It's dangerous of course, but as we join Thomas in his adventurous call to go with Jesus to death, where life awaits on the other side, we go in Jesus' power and assurance that he is with us every step of the way, as we become living proclamations of worship and witness to the world for God's glory.[125]

We have no firm historical evidence from which we can learn what happened to Thomas after the ascension of

Jesus, but church tradition records him taking the gospel to India and establishing the church in south Asia before being martyred.[126] Whatever actually happened, there is no doubt that Thomas and his friends changed the world forever as they responded to their resurrected Lord by worshipfully living and proclaiming the gospel in his power wherever they went.

As we encounter the risen Jesus for ourselves, how will we respond?

May it be no less than a declaration of 'my Lord and my God' with our lips and our lives, to a world who don't yet know the hope and joy of true worship, so that by God's grace all may move from a moment of doubt to an eternity of devotion.

CHAPTER SIX: DISCUSSION QUESTIONS

How does the thought of engaging in evangelism make you feel?

Do you ever struggle with comparison?

Have you seen people come to faith through sharing with them, are you still waiting for the fruit of other encounters?

If God asked you right now, 'Are you available to me?' what would your answer be?

CHAPTER SIX: APPLICATION

Visit **advancegroups.org** and think about starting an Advance group at your church or with some friends as you look to answer the adventurous call that God has for your life with a resounding 'Here I am Lord, I'm available.'

ACKNOWLEDGEMENTS

Thanks to my Message family. It is a joy to be a part of a truly Jesus-centred prayer and proclamation movement, and I am especially thankful to Andy Hawthorne, Sam Ward and Ian Rowbottom for their leadership, wisdom and friendship, as well as my Advance colleagues Luiz Cardoso and Peter Thompson.

Likewise, Kevin, Andrew and the rest of the Palau team, not least my co-editor on this series Des Henry, I could not wish to have better partners to walk with, I thank you for your brotherly love and constant encouragement.

Thanks to Jamie Hill and the team at Kingsway CLC Trust for their trust in me and their belief in this book and the Advance Proclaimers series as a whole. Thank you for your hard work and for taking such care to bring it to publication in the way you have.

To all who read the manuscript and offered feedback and advice, I am indebted to you improving this book in numerous ways, particularly Des, Sam, Luiz and my old man (or Chris as most know him).

Thanks as ever to Simon Baker for moulding the book into its final readable shape. Any remaining mistakes or poor attempts at humour are entirely my own responsibility.

To my family – you are more of a blessing to me than I could ever express.

Thank you above all to my Lord and my God.

ABOUT THE AUTHOR

Ben Jack is the global head of Advance, based at The Message Trust (**message.org.uk**) in Manchester, England. Ben travels the world to preach the gospel and encourage and equip others to do likewise. He is the author of *The Simple Gospel* and *The Advance Group Mentoring Guide* and has been known to produce music and tour as the DJ Galactus Jack. Ben and his wife Naomi live in Manchester with their pug Toshi.

NOTES

1   We'll leave the eternal triune God in his own category when thinking of favourites!

2   2 Kings 2:23-25.

3   After all, pessimism and evangelism go together about as well as Manchester United and Liverpool fans (or Yankees and Red Sox for my American friends).

4   He only gets a mention in the apostolic lists of the synoptic gospels (Matthew 10:3; Mark 3:18; Luke 6:15; also Acts 1:13), but he plays more of a role in John's gospel (11:16; 14:5; 20:24-28; 21:2).

5   'It is difficult, perhaps unwise, to weave full-blown character types out of the meagre information the gospels give us about the men and women who followed Jesus. Thomas is a case in point… Not too much to build upon. Perhaps we can tentatively conjecture a loyal but somewhat unimaginative person who will act only on what he is sure of.' Bruce Milne, *The Message of John: Here Is Your King! with Study Guide, The Bible Speaks Today* (Leicester, England; Downers Grove, IL: InterVarsity Press, 1993), 302.

6   *Indiana Jones and the Temple of Doom* reference: all present and correct.

7   I bet you don't know what his real name is either, even if you've seen the film multiple times!

8   Okay, you definitely thought Rocky was his real name, didn't you? Nope, it's Robert. Oh and Tom Cruise in *Top Gun*? Pete Mitchell. Yes, seriously. No offence if you're a Pete, but Maverick is way cooler.

9   Matthew 14:31; 28:17; Mark 16:11; Luke 24:11.

10   Not a nickname that we find in the Bible but one that has developed through church tradition.

11   Jennifer Michael Hecht, *Doubt: A History* (New York: Harper Collins, 2003), 493-494.

12   Isaiah 1:18, 1 Peter 3:15.

13   1 Corinthians 13:12.

14   Romans 12:12.

15   Genesis 3:1.

16   1 Samuel 13:5–14.

17   Matthew 16:16.

18   Matthew 7:12.

19   Luke 22:42–44.

20   John 8:36; Galatians 5:1.

21   Psalm 147: 4–5; Ephesians 3:20; 2 Timothy 1:7.

22   Isaiah 25:1; Psalm 100:5; Joshua 1:9; Proverbs 3:5–6.

23   Matthew 6:33.

24   Jude 22

25   Psalm 34:8; Matthew 11:28.

NOTES

26 'Blessed, then, are those who cannot share Thomas' experience of sight, but who, in part because they read of Thomas' experience, come to share Thomas' faith.' D. A. Carson, *The Gospel according to John, The Pillar New Testament Commentary* (Leicester, England; Grand Rapids, MI: Inter-Varsity Press; W.B. Eerdmans, 1991), 660.

27 Romans 5:8.

28 Luke 23:34.

29 John 14:6.

30 Romans 5:5.

31 Ravi Zacharias and Abdu M, *Seeing Jesus from the East* (Grand Rapids: Zondervan, 2020) 73.

32 John 1:12.

33 'The death of Jesus was such an overwhelming reality that he must get alone to try and come to terms with it. So when Jesus comes to the disciples on the Easter evening, Thomas is not there.' Milne, *The Message of John*, 302.

34 Google it.

35 J. M. Comer, *The Ruthless Elimination of Hurry* (Colorado Springs: Waterbrook Press, 2019).

36 Elena Blanco-Suarez, "The Effects of Solitary Confinement on the Brain: Neurobiology shows the need to make solitary confinement more humane," *Psychology Today*, February 27, 2019, <https://www.psychologytoday.com/gb/blog/brain-chemistry/201902/the-effects-solitary-confinement-the-brain>

37 Terry Waite, *Taken on Trust: 25th Anniversary Edition* (London: Hodder & Stoughton, 2016), Kindle edition.

38   John T. Cacioppo and William Patrick, *Loneliness: Human Nature and the Need for Social Connection* (New York: W. W. Norton & Company, 2008), Kindle Edition.

39   Murthy, Vivek H., *Together* (London: Profile, 2020), Kindle edition.

40   Richard E. Cytowic, "Does Loneliness Eat at You? Screen Media May Be to Blame: The instant gratification of tech stunts your ability to connect and empathize.," *Psychology Today*, January 22, 2020 <https://www.psychologytoday.com/gb/blog/the-fallible-mind/202001/does-loneliness-eat-you-screen-media-may-be-blame>

41   Blanco-Suarez, "The Neuroscience of Loneliness".

42   There is one God: Deuteronomy 6:4. Expressed in three Persons: 1 John 5:7; Matthew 28:19. Each is equally divine: John 20:28; Colossians 2:9; Job 33:4; 2 Corinthians 3:3, 17. For a short but thorough explanation of basic trinitarian theology see R.C. Sproul, *What is the Trinity? Crucial Questions Series Book 10* (Sanford FL: Reformation Trust Publishing, 2011).

43   'The worst solitude is to be destitute of sincere friendship.'

44   Ecclesiastes 4:9–12.

45   Dietrich Bonhoeffer, *Life Together and Prayerbook of the Bible*, ed. Gerhard Ludwig Müller, Albrecht Schönherr, and Geffrey B. Kelly, trans. Daniel W. Bloesch and James H. Burtness, vol. 5, Dietrich Bonhoeffer Works (Minneapolis, MN: Fortress Press, 1996), 110.

46   Hopefully this happens graciously, but we all have that one staggeringly undiplomatic and unfiltered friend. Then again, grace is a two-way street and God is always helping us grow. Yes, even through that friend.

NOTES

47　'In the ancient world there was virtually no such thing as private life. A tiny number of the aristocracy or the very rich were able to afford a measure of privacy. But for the great majority, life was lived publicly and visibly. The streets were mostly narrow, the houses and tenements were mostly cramped, there was noise and smell everywhere, and everybody knew everybody else's business.' Tom Wright, *Paul: A Biography* (London: SPCK, 2018), Kindle edition.

48　Orson Welles, *Someone to Love* (1987 film) words added by Welles to Henry Jaglom's script.

49　Psalm 139.

50　Matthew 1:23.

51　It's not that my parents weren't generous, they were, but even as a young teenager I understood the reality of financial limitation in our household.

52　C.S. Lewis, *A Grief Observed* (London: Faber & Faber, Readers Edition, 2014), Kindle Edition.

53　See Craig S. Keener, *The Gospel of John: A Commentary, vol. 1* (Grand Rapids, MI: Baker Academic, 2012), 1209.

54　'The reality is that you will grieve forever. You will not "get over" the loss of a loved one; you will learn to live with it. You will heal and you will rebuild yourself around the loss you have suffered. You will be whole again but you will never be the same.' Elisabeth Kübler-Ross and David Kessler, *On Grief and Grieving: Finding the meaning of grief through the five stages of loss* (London: Simon and Schuster, 2005), 230.

55　John 4:48.

56 Hebrews 11:1. 'The faith celebrated in 11:1–40 is characterized
    by firmness, reliability, and steadfastness. It is trust in God and in
    his promises (cf. 4:1–3; 6:1; 11:6, 17–19, 29). The context shows
    that what these attested witnesses affirm is the reliability of God,
    who is faithful to his promise (11:11). Committing themselves
    to God who is steadfast, these exemplars of faith were themselves
    made steadfast.' William L. Lane, *Hebrews 9–13, vol. 47B,
    Word Biblical Commentary* (Dallas: Word, Incorporated, 1991),
    315–316.

57 A great example of 'examining the evidence' can be found in J.
    Warner Wallace's *Cold Case Christianity: A Homicide Detective
    Investigates the Claims of the Gospels* (Colorado Springs: David C.
    Cook, 2013).

58 Grant R. Osborne, *John: Verse by Verse*, ed. Jeffrey Reimer et al.,
    Osborne New Testament Commentaries (Bellingham, WA:
    Lexham Press, 2018), 469.

59 John 2:23–25.

60 Although the Greek word *eirēnē* is used for peace here, rather
    than the Hebrew word *shalom*, the idea is the same. The New
    Testament writers commonly use the word *eirēnē* to convey the
    Old Testament concept of *shalom*.

61 This is my wording and not an exact definition. There are a
    few ways in which *shalom* can be explained and used but they
    ultimately all point in the same direction and the Bible confirms
    shalom to be a word that beautifully sums up God's desire for his
    creation: wholeness, wellness, balance, fulfilment – things as they
    should be by his will and power.

62 Milne, *The Message of John*, 297.

NOTES

63 Yuval Noah Harari discuses some of these points in his book *Homo Deus: A Brief History of Tomorrow* (London: Vintage, 2017) in which, for example, he asserts that you are now more likely to commit suicide than die in war. The challenges may have changed, but the chaos remains.

64 Michel Chion, *BFI Modern Classics: The Thin Red Line* (London: BFI Publishing, 2004) 33.

65 Lewis, *A Grief Observed.*

66 Rebecca Manley Pippert, *Stay Salt: The World Has Changed, Our Message Must Not* (Epsom: The Good Book Company, 2020), Kindle edition.

67 2 Corinthians 5:21.

68 R. C. Sproul, *John, St. Andrew's Expositional Commentary*, 390. © Ligonier Ministries, Inc. 2009. Used by permission of Ligonier Ministries, Inc.

69 2 Peter 3:10.

70 Matthew 6:9–10.

71 John 1:14; John 14:2; 1 Thessalonians 4:16-17.

72 See Hebrews 11:10, 16; Revelation 21.

73 Psalm 145:13; Romans 14:17; Galatians 5:22-23; see also Matthew 13.

74 Acts 7:55–56; We no longer feel at home in this fallen world having now become citizens of heaven (Philippians 3:20), but we follow in the steps of our Lord by staying here for a time to be ambassadors of the perfect kingdom and bring its light to the world (2 Corinthians 5:20). Along the way we are daily transformed by God's grace, renewed in preparation for the full glory of heaven, the new world that awaits (Philippians 1:6; 3:21).

75 Tom Wright, *God and the Pandemic* (London: SPCK, 2020), Kindle edition.

76 It's a metaphor, don't take me to task for failing to observe the rules of symphonic structure!

77 See Colin G. Kruse, *John: An Introduction and Commentary, vol. 4, Tyndale New Testament Commentaries* (Downers Grove, IL: InterVarsity Press, 2003), 379.

78 See Sproul, *John*, 393.

79 Revelation 4:11.

80 Suetonius, *The Twelve Ceasars: Domitian*, 13.

81 Just as Jesus doesn't demand worship by the disciples in the boat having walked on water, but Matthew informs us that they bowed down before (worshipped) him when he got into the boat (Matthew 14:33). It is hard to know what this 'worship' was exactly, as these good young Jews would only have truly worshipped God, and they surely did not perceive Jesus to be God at that time. Perhaps Matthew, writing his gospel years after the event, was able to make sense of their instinctive yet at the time confusing action of bowing before Jesus as 'worship' in light of now knowing him to be God himself. In any event, the point remains that Thomas is the first to directly call Jesus God (a profession of worship), and in both examples the worship is offered not in response to a demand from Jesus, but in response to who he is.

82 'Thomas' utterance cannot possibly be taken as shocked profanity addressed to God (if to anyone), a kind of blasphemous version of a stunned "My word!"… such profanity would not have been

found in first-century Palestine on the lips of a devout Jew.'
Carson, *John*, 658.

83 When Peter steps up to preach the first Christian sermon at
Pentecost, the Lordship of Jesus as the fulfilment of what God
has promised is the centrepiece of it all (Acts 2:21). God has done
what he promised he would do, and he has done it through Jesus,
Messiah, King of Kings, Lord and God.

84 Romans 10:9.

85 G. Beasley-Murray, *John (Word Biblical Commentary)* (Grand
Rapids: Zondervan, 2012), 385–386. Copyright © 2012 by
George Beasley-Murray. Used by permission of Zondervan. www.
zondervan.com.

86 Ephesians 2:10.

87 I find that Manchester United fans also qualify.

88 Rowan Williams, *God With Us: The Meaning Of The Cross And
Resurrection – Then And Now*, (London: SPCK, 2017), Kindle
edition. Or in the words of A. W. Tozer, 'worship originates with
God and comes back to us and is reflected from us, as a mirror.
God accepts no other kind of worship.' A.W. Tozer, *Whatever
Happened to Worship?* (Camp Hill, PN: Wingspread, 2012),
Kindle edition.

89 From a sermon entitled, 'The Sin of Omission', 1955.

90 Find out more at **www.pocmin.com**.

91 Tozer, *Whatever Happened To Worship?*

92 One of the reasons something like The Alpha Course
(**www.alpha.org**) has been so successful is that it creates space for
people to ask questions and get to the heart of Christian truth,
whether you're already a Christian or someone exploring faith.

93   Psalm 19:7–8.

94   Matthew 4:4.

95   Lois Tverberg, *Reading the Bible with Rabbi Jesus* (Grand Rapids: Baker, 2017), Kindle edition. '...everyone seems to be into "artisanal" foods. They want to savor authentic flavors, taste food from centuries-old recipes. They love organic cheeses and heirloom vegetables, farmers' markets and food co-ops. People want to eat slow food, not fast food. It takes more time and effort, but it's worth it, they say. You know what? I'm into artisanal Bible study.'

96   Luke 24:13–35.

97   James R. Edwards, *The Gospel according to Luke, The Pillar New Testament Commentary* (Grand Rapids; Cambridge; Nottingham, Eerdmans; Apollos, 2015), 720–721.

98   Ever heard the acronym Basic Instructions Before Leaving Earth used to describe the Bible? It's cute but it misses the point. The Bible is not there to work merely as an instruction manual for life, but to actually introduce you to the living instruction himself by way of telling you his story.

99   2 Timothy 2:1–13.

100   Matthew 4:1–11.

101   Ephesians 6:10–17.

102   John 12:16. Also see back to my point in note 81.

103   Hebrews 4:12.

104   Brian Moynahan, *William Tyndale: If God Spare My Life* (London: Abacus, 2002) 31.

105   The remarkable work of Open Doors and Voice of the Martyrs continues to this day, visit **opendoors.org** and **persecution.com** respectively.

NOTES

106 Richard Wurmbrand, *Tortured for Christ* (London: Hodder & Stoughton, 2004). Incidentally, as a young woman my mum once had to drive Richard Wurmbrand to a speaking engagement. Nervous at transporting someone she admired so much, she almost had an accident with him in the car. Richard, with a twinkle in his eye, introduced his sermon that evening by saying, 'Many people have tried to kill me over the years, but no-one has come as close as this young lady!'

107 Brother Yun with Paul Hattaway, *The Heavenly Man* (Oxford: Lion Hudson, 2002) 28.

108 Yun, *Heavenly Man*, 29.

109 Shūsaku Endō, *Silence*, (New Jersey: Taplinger, 1969) 190–191.

110 Zacharias, *Seeing Jesus from the East*, 83.

111 I highly recommend the 2018 documentary, but be warned, even if you know how it turns out, the final twenty minutes will leave you without any fingernails.

112 If the recommendation of *Free Solo* leaves you wanting something even more stomach churning, seek out Aron Ralston's book *127 Hours: Between a Rock and a Hard Place* (London: Simon & Schuster, 2004) or the Danny Boyle film of the same name (2011).

113 Or translated from the German more literally, 'Whenever Christ calls us, his call leads us to death.' Dietrich Bonhoeffer, *Discipleship*, ed. Martin Kuske et al., trans. Barbara Green and Reinhard Krauss, vol. 4, Dietrich Bonhoeffer Works (Minneapolis, MN: Fortress Press, 2003), 87.

114 Matthew 16:25; Luke 17:33.

115 John 11:25–26.

116 'Gospel ninja' is just a theological term for an evangelist.

117 Acts 4:13.

118 Quoted in Mark Galli and Ted Olsen, *131 Christians Everyone Should Know* (Nashville, TN: Broadman & Holman Publishers, 2000), 245. Reprinted and used by permission.

119 A paraphrase of her actual words from one of my very favourite missionary life stories, Gladys Aylward, *Gladys Aylward: The Little Woman* (Chicago: Moody Publishers, 1974), Kindle Edition.

120 Aylward, *The Little Woman*.

121 Wright, *Paul: A Biography*.

122 Genesis 9:11–13.

123 Mark 2:1–12.

124 Aylward, *The Little Woman*.

125 Acts 1:8; Matthew 28:20.

126 The St Thomas Cathedral Basilica in Chennai was built over the purported location of Thomas' tomb in India, and on St Thomas Mount – where it is believed that the apostle was martyred around AD 72 – you can find various inscriptions of 'my Lord and my God' around the shrine and surrounding area which draws thousands of pilgrims each year. While we may not know the exact details of Thomas' death, one thing we do know is that he *didn't* write the Gospel of Thomas, a gnostic text that doesn't meet the criteria for inclusion in the biblical canon: apostolic authority (it is dated too late to be written by Thomas, mid-second century); divine qualities (it contradicts other NT texts); church acceptance (it was rejected by the early church as being heretical).

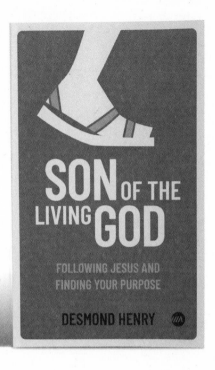

ALSO IN THE ADVANCE PROCLAIMERS SERIES

Son of the Living God: Following Jesus and finding your purpose

by Desmond Henry

COMING SOON

THE GOSPEL. THERE IS NO PLAN B.

The gospel is good news to be proclaimed and has lost none of its power to save. Through small group mentoring, Advance equips, encourages and empowers the church in evangelism while also stirring and developing evangelistic gifting in those called as evangelists.

Advance grew out of a commitment by British and American evangelists Andy Hawthorne (The Message Trust) and Andrew Palau (Luis Palau Association) to gather up to twelve younger preaching evangelists in small group community to intentionally develop and sharpen them. Since its inception in 2015, Advance has grown from the first group in Manchester, UK, to a global movement of hundreds of groups meeting regularly around the world who are committed to fanning into flame the gift of God in their lives that the world may know him.

FIVE PRINCIPLES OF THE MOVEMENT
- ⏱ Regular meeting
- ✂ Sharpening
- 🔍 Accountability
- 💬 Communication
- ✗ Multiplication

Advance exists to increase and equip the number of Christians who will unashamedly put the lamp of the gospel on a stand around the globe, be it from a platform or through daily encounters with family, friends or even strangers.

Discover more and sign up to start a group:

ADVANCEGROUPS.ORG

ADVANCE GROUP
MENTORING GUIDE

Your 72-page guide featuring everything you need to start an
Advance Group and session discussion materials for the first year.

ADVANCEGROUPS.ORG

GLOBAL NETWORK OF ΞVANGELISTS

SO THAT ALL MAY HEAR //

One evangelist can reach only so far. One organization can do only so much. By working together, we multiply our efforts for the expansion of the Gospel. This is the vision of our Global Network of Evangelists.

Dedicating the next decade to accelerate evangelism worldwide, the Palau Association is working to build networks of evangelists in 150 countries. These networks are being developed through strong, trusted relationships with evangelists and Christian organizations around the globe, with a vision to connect and encourage evangelists as never before to win more people to Christ.

This Global Network of Evangelists is using all available means to annually reach millions with the good news of Jesus Christ. What God is doing through this outstanding network of evangelists is truly astounding.

LUIS PALAU

Through mentoring and equipping, collaborative outreach events, and training and conferences, members are provided with the help they need to impact their world for Christ. Our plan is to extend this offering to thousands more evangelists from around the world, forming the first-ever global network, spread across 150+ countries.

evangelist.global

Equipping the Church

Equipping the Church exists to do just that, equip the church for all areas of ministry.

If you are an evangelist, you, and anyone else in your church with any area of responsibility and leadership, can become an Equip member and receive the following long term benefits:

- 20% off orders in-store and online*
- Special offers at event bookstores
- Regular e-newsletters about new church resources
- Seasonal brochures highlighting key books and resources

*some exclusions apply, such as packs that are already discounted and some sale items

This scheme is designed to help you access the best resources to equip you and your church for ministry and evangelism.

Please go to **www.equippingthechurch.com/equip** to sign up now!

"SO THAT THE
SERVANT OF GOD
MAY BE THOROUGHLY
EQUIPPED FOR EVERY
GOOD WORK."
2 TIMOTHY 3:17

a ministry partnership initiative from CLC

2 TIMOTHY 3:17

Name: MR J SMITH
Church: CITY EVANGELICAL CHURCH
Account: 0123 4567 8901 234
Expires: 04/2021